# The Invisible Breath.....

## ......That Breathes All of Life

# The Invisible Breath.....

## ......That Breathes All of Life

## Heidi Lorenz

DANCING MOON PRESS
NEWPORT. OREGON

The Invisible Breath.…That Breathes All of Life
**copyright © 2011 by Heidi Lorenz**
**All rights reserved**

Lorenz, Heidi
*The Invisible Breath.… That Breathes All of Life*
1. Title; 2. Metaphysics; 3. Mysticism; 4. Spiritual Life; 5. Feminine Wisdom

ISBN-13: 978-1-892076-88-5
Library of Congress Control Number: 2011920834
Manufactured in the United States of America

*Cover and interior illustrations by* Heidi Lorenz
*Book design:* Carla Perry, Dancing Moon Press
*Cover design & production:* Jana Westhusing, StudioBlue West


DANCING MOON PRESS
P.O. Box 832, Newport, OR 97365
541-574-7708
www.dancingmoonpress.com
info@dancingmoonpress.com

**FIRST EDITION**

The inspiration for this book rises out of
the heart that Loves all that Is.
The dedication is to Absolute Truth
that holds all things as One.
The invitation is to return to the Essence of your being,
which is Love itself.

# Contents

# Introduction

The intention of this book is to assist through wisdom, storytelling, poetry and art the journey back to our essence. The blank pages invite the reader to become a part of the story, no longer separate from what is unfolding within and upon the planet. Our life experiences help us awaken through our sensate bodies to the present moment. This is possible when we stop separating from our feelings and from what is occurring in the moment of our experience.

The Earth and all of its magnificent creatures are part of this experience. Man has created an elaborate illusion to separate Spirit from Matter. This has resulted in a false sense of power and control over the physical world of Matter. This damaging and painful illusion has created not only unhealthy ecological conditions, but also unhealthy relationships with all of life—even our physical bodies. In our unconscious state, we may continue to destroy what supports our physical existence: both our bodies and the Earth herself. With conscious awakening, we can use free will to make different choices.

Awakening is painful, but it is necessary to experience this precious life as it is happening. From a mystical viewpoint, destruction and creation are both forces of LOVE held within the Divine Being of the cosmos. It is an illusion that we are separate from these forces. We are part of the creation and the destruction occurring upon the planet. The gift is to say "yes" to the experience of life that holds all things as one.

The hope is that what is contained in this book is read and felt through the human heart, which allows "love to flow no matter what." It is this flow through our heart that holds all things as one—our pain and joy, love and hate, creation and destruction. The human heart knows all things are one, and to be held within this heart allows us to experience life fully. It allows us to make choices that are no longer self-centered, but to include all of life. This vision is not part of the dualistic view of the world that separates Spirit and Matter, but of a view that sees and experiences the interconnectedness of all life.

Please indulge this writer and try to experience what lies within these pages with your heart, opening your mind beyond its current limitations and beliefs. To experience life beyond the constructs of the mind allows humans to have direct experiences of the Divine, which is constantly recreating itself. We are part of this Divine Being and witness to its creation and destruction. It is a gift to experience fully. Witnessing is being part of the beauty of a sunset as the sun moves below the horizon and out of sight, creating darkness. We know it will always rise again.

It is within the darkness of the unknown that all life is created and woven together by an invisible web of light. The current Western mind has separated itself from the physical world, desiring to direct life and death upon the planet, and yielding a false sense of safety. It has forgotten that humans, as well as all life, are part of creation rising out of the unknown. The stories within these pages are simple life experiences any human being might have. They have been lived through a heart desiring Truth and Understanding by way of the physical experience of life rather than the separation from it. A continued awakening progresses and is illustrated through these stories. Physical life is such a gift, and it has been given to all of us in order "To Be Known" within its current form.

While reading the stories and poems, include yourself by witnessing your own life experiences as part of the web of life. Use the blank pages for notes, your own poems, dreams, or drawings. Find ways to be conscious of "the breath of life" breathing you. Remember to ask yourself, How can I create harmony in my home environment, my work environment, within nature herself? How can I better connect with Life-giving energies? How might I become a part of life and contribute through connection? These efforts come when we feel gratitude in our hearts rather than the never-ending desires of the ego.

This book can be used in book clubs, women's groups, anywhere it can assist with facilitating inner and outer connections. It is given in service to the whole of life with deep gratitude for all experiences contained within it.

# The Call

In the silence of the mind
One can hear the sound
Of the heart ushering you
        Home

It is a constant hum
That echoes in the silence
Resonating with a deep and
        Ancient Truth

As the silence brings complete stillness
The vibration brings
A new awareness of the
Essential nature of life

We are all One
Within the Divine Being of life
Unfolding its beauty into
The light of Day

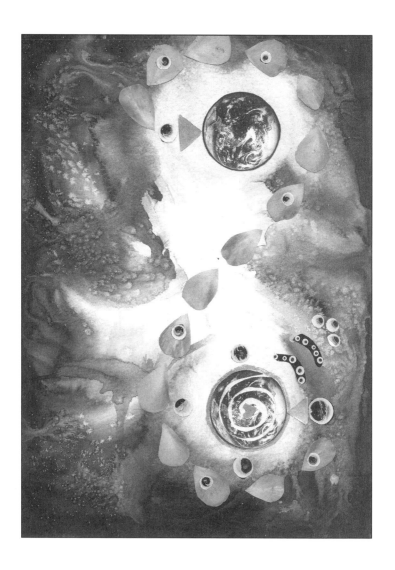

# Two Worlds

The world of light and
The world of matter

One full of life
The other solid and hard

One moving and flowing
The other fixed and conceived

One able to breathe and change
The other dead and lifeless

Once the two worlds were one
They were separated by fear

And dominated by control.

Welcome to a story where the storyteller and the story are one. Rita is born six pounds five ounces in a small hospital in upstate New York. In these days, they often put women to sleep during childbirth, separating them from the process. New techniques and procedures are being invented all the time to produce an acceptable outcome to a process that has always been natural to women—childbirth. In a brightly lit, sterile room, rank with the smell of rubbing alcohol, Rita's soul is birthed into the physical world.

Cold sharp metal forceps firmly grip her head to pull Rita through the invisible barrier within the birth canal of her mother. This barrier separates the spiritual world from the physical world and is connected only through Breath.

The womb of the woman is a place where magic happens: the unseen becomes visible through form and is then birthed into the manifest world. Rita's right eye is focused inward, toward spirit. Her left eye is focused on the outer world. This physical anomaly causes the right eye to cross the midline toward the nose, unable to focus on the outer world, while the left eye tracks activities in the world. Rita's mother Millie is shown exercises to help strengthen Rita's eye, so it can focus and connect with the happenings in the external environment. Millie works with Rita daily to strengthen the eye muscles, training her right eye to move into the center of the socket and face outward so it can see the world.

Even in infancy, Rita recognizes the separation of the spiritual world from the physical one and cries inconsolably. Millie attempts to comfort Rita, but nothing but sleep appeases the cry of her soul for Spirit. The little body that houses Rita's soul knows only that it is separate from something it loves.

Rita's brother, Peter, is nine months older, with bright red hair. He competes for their parent's attention and affection. This does not bring the siblings together; it drives a wedge of jealousy between them. Peter is searching for something, but he never finds it where he looks. Whatever he's looking for eludes him, and Rita represents something he hungers for but cannot find in food or relationships.

Rita is a shy little girl with brown curly hair, big brown eyes, and an average build. Outwardly, she blends in with other five-year-olds. But inside, Rita feels the body and the physical world as heavy, sticky, as if she's walking around in mud. Each step taken in the physical world adds another layer of mud. Rita feels as though her legs are caked to the knees with mud. This is an unpleasant physical sensation, but it is Rita's first impression of herself within the physical world.

Rita doesn't understand the world of grownups. Her favorite part of the world is the ground—feeling moss squish under her feet, smelling the dampness of the dirt. She imagines herself four inches tall, walking among salamanders and other critters she knows only as her relatives. She is not afraid of anything in the natural world. The creatures are part of her and Rita loves them all. Here in nature, Rita experiences herself differently—not heavy or separate, but part of her surroundings, surroundings that support her physical body and soul.

Rita, wishing to be close to the earth, takes up eating

dirt out of the houseplants, upsetting Millie enough so that she removes all the houseplants from Rita's reach. Millie is concerned with the welfare of her children and wants no harm to come to them. There are many rules in Rita's house, and of course, the enforcer of the rules is Rita's father, Ralph. Ralph has a strong German accent, piercing clear blue eyes, and light brown hair. He is passionate about whatever he is involved with and this passion ignites into fury when something interferes with his direction. Rita both fears and adores her father, which sets up a strong inner conflict of the opposites—love and hate.

NEVER LEAVE THE TABLE UNTIL ALL THE FOOD IS EATEN.

This is one of the strictest rules in Rita's house. Upon occasion, Rita sits at the table until 10 p.m., especially when it is liver and onions night, her most dreaded meal. She tries everything—holding her breath and swallowing, washing it down with milk, hiding the food in napkins—but sometimes it is just a struggle of wills, Ralph verses Rita. Rita's father, Ralph, is adamant that no food go to waste. He says often enough how he lived through some of the hardest, poorest years in Germany during and after World War II. He tells stories of how he was sent out to beg for food for the family from neighbors and would return with an egg and a potato that had to be shared among four people, always leaving their bellies unsatisfied.

As a five-year-old, Rita knows only that she hates liver and onions and doesn't understand why she is forced to eat something she hates. There are always chores to do and children are expected to assist in all yard work, clear the table, do the dishes, pick up their rooms and be on time.

Rules and chores are part of the structure Rita learns. Games and playtime are in second place. This seems natural to Rita, for it is how her house is run. Both Rita's parents are intelligent and college-educated—her father with a Ph.D. in physics, her mother with a B.S. in Biology—and both place a high priority on education for their children.

Church and religion are available but not required, except on religious holidays like Christmas and Easter. Ralph says he does not believe in organized religion and Rita is not sure if her father even believes in a God. He makes statements like, "What kind of a God would have allowed the Nazis to do what they did in Germany?"He is vague when it comes to his spiritual beliefs.

Rita's mother is compelled to expose her children to Christianity, something she was brought up with. Millie is a small woman, barely five feet tall with a tiny bone structure. She has short brown hair and hazel eyes lit by her intelligence. She follows outer society norms, not knowing any other way to be.

Dressed in a navy blue and white dress, Rita sits in a stone church with arched, stained-glass windows and hard wooden benches. The scenes in the stained glass don't interest Rita, but the colors do. She loves purple and indigo blue and her eyes search out those hues. A man is in front wearing a black gown and purple scarf with golden crosses on the ends. Rita listens to the tone of the man's voice but does not understand his words. Her heart is not attracted to him or the way the church feels. She does not feel any warmth in the people of the church; even when they sing it feels as if something precious is missing. Rita gazes out the window and her heart longs for a connection. She sees a beautiful oak tree and thinks, "I would feel so much closer to God outside under the branches of the tree, smelling the fresh air, and feeling the sun upon my skin." Rita learns how to live in the world of grownups but never relinquishes the place inside that keeps her connected to nature and what seems most real to her.

# Awareness

Awaken to the environment
Through the body and our senses,

Smell, sight, sound, taste
Touch and inner vision,

Using the breath to connect...
The outer environment
To the inner wisdom,

Putting us into the moment
Where new possibilities exist
And realities can change.

In the beginning, school is difficult for Rita. She and her brother Peter are in the same grade, but never in the same classroom until their algebra class in high school. At home, Rita and Peter are treated the same by their parents, Ralph and Millie, despite their sexual orientation. They are expected to perform equally at home and in school. Rita doesn't see herself as incapable because she is a girl, or different from her brother. Rita forms without gender-related limitations or constraints generally found in the collective unconscious. Outwardly, she appears as a tomboy; inwardly she does not recognize differences between the sexes.

Second grade is the turning point for Rita. Her second grade teacher, Ms. Anderson, sees something in Rita that no one else sees. Ms. Anderson is a six-foot-tall black angel with a turquoise dress and large wings. Rita feels safe with Ms. Anderson, but not elsewhere at school. Rita can't identify what is threatening her body, but school is not like the peaceful harmony of nature. Her sensate awareness is keen to the emotional chaos in the classroom and the pressures of individuated wills developing. Love and acceptance are invisible but felt through the heart. These nutrients pour through the classroom from Ms. Anderson and nurture something deep in Rita's heart, making her less shy and more secure in the school environment.

School starts becoming easier for Rita, and she begins performing well in class and socializing with other kids. She begins to find out more of who she is as years pass, filling her with the experiences that life brings. While Rita is in high school, she and her family move to the West Coast from New York. The East Coast has Rita's extended family—aunts, uncles, cousins, grandparents and the German culture from Europe, both enriching and enmeshing. Cultures and families have engrained patterns and rituals that are automatic and unconscious. People are comfortable with their patterns. The patterns are like grooves in a record that provide direction for people and guide their choices. The patterns are unseen structures that weave people's lives together in the physical world, but do not always support and nurture their inner experience. This happens so subtly that most people are unaware it is occurring until they become completely separate from the living-breathing experience of life.

But not for Rita. Rita is aware that what she is feeling and sensing within her heart is not always what the physical world is visibly expressing. This causes misunderstandings, but Rita refuses to relinquish her experience to conform to the dictates of the outer world. As a child and young adult, this is painful for Rita. Something inside—as imperceptible as a whisper—guides Rita to stay connected to life even with its painful misunderstandings. This gentle guidance is always with Rita. It helps to keep her awake within the physical world of the unconscious.

The West Coast is devoid of extended family illuminating the outer structures, which decreases the power of these unconscious patterns and makes changes easier for Rita's family. There are fewer outer structures holding Rita's family in place in California. They experience a freedom to move beyond the restrictions of set patterns and create their own new experiences. Her father decides to have an extramarital affair after meeting a woman on a trip back to the East Coast. Subsequently, Ralph blames Millie for not meeting his needs as a partner, both sexually and emotionally.

The news is crippling to Rita's mother, Millie, who has given up her own aspirations to support her husband's dreams. Millie graduated at the top of her class in biology at an Ivy League school and continued on to Johns Hopkins for her nursing certification. Ralph and Millie met in Europe after the war, and Millie supported Ralph through a Ph.D. program in physics at a technical school in New York. Most individuals look to the outside world to guide their lives, not recognizing that what they see are dreams and patterns of a collective reality, not their own dreams that are asleep within their hearts. This takes more than intelligence; it takes someone being awake and present to themselves and the unfolding reality.

It is common to hear of men who feel unfulfilled in their middle years and blame it on the woman in their lives. Men are usually unaware that they are projecting their own inner feminine onto an externalized woman leaving. They feel empty, both inside their bodies and within their marriage. Often, men and women neglect their own inner wisdom in order to feel safe in the outside world, becoming experts in controlling and manipulating rather than finding their own wisdom and power. The tension within Rita's household is building between Ralph and Millie. Rita's father does not remember life as something warm, kind, generous or loving due to his experiences growing up in Germany before and after World War II. To him, life is harsh, cold, and insufficient to meet his basic needs for love, nourishment, and safety.

Most children growing up in Germany during this period experienced similar hardships, but how they respond to those hardships determined how they respond to life later on. Ralph has difficulty seeing himself separate from what he endured in Germany. For him, life is not rich with love, which makes it difficult for him to express love. He experiences his life as hard and believes one must work hard to get anything. This is his view of life, and it covers him and everyone around him with its austere landscape. Ralph's relationships with others continue to mirror his early experiences. Not only does he have to work hard to get acknowledgement and appreciation, but he does not give out acknowledgement easily. He cannot separate his original life experiences from what he lives now. This is so fixed, with so little possibility for change, that he often says, "People don't change," and "I can't change."

Rita, Peter and her younger sister Joyce are subjected to the same harsh treatment Ralph endured as a child due to his unconscious patterning behavior.

One evening, Rita, her brother and sister, and some neighborhood children are playing Hide-and-Seek at dusk in their yard. They have spent a good part of the day helping Ralph put in an underground sprinkler system in the yard. The job is not complete—exposed pipes and sprinkler heads can easily be stepped on or kicked over.

After the game, Ralph yells out to Rita, Peter, and Joyce, 'Who kicked over the sprinkler head?' All three respond, 'Not me! I didn't do it.' Ralph begins to rant. His voice explodes with anger. He loses control. His eyes become daggers piercing each child, searing their skin. He intends to scare the truth out of them. This is a familiar performance to all the children, for they have witnessed this behavior many times. They look at each other with dread, knowing some form of punishment is coming. But Rita feels strength and fierceness within her as she walks behind Ralph into the garage, where he grabs a ski pole. Rita's brother is always first, then Rita, and then her sister. This has always been the sequence. Domination and control are the most important tactics during these episodes. Bend over, whap… whap… whap… is the sound of the ski pole sailing through the air as it lands hard and furious on the backsides of Rita and her siblings.

In the midst of the third whap, an electric current flips a switch in Rita's mind and she hears, "There is something wrong here. It is not okay to hit children." Rita spins around and yells at her father, tears streaming down her cheeks, "You hit me again and I'm calling the police, packing my bags and leaving."

The words stop all activity. The air is electric and the moment is illuminated. A pattern is broken and Ralph never lays another hand on Rita.

Much later, when Rita is in her thirties, Ralph apologizes for hitting her as a child. He has no memory of beating his children, but Rita's mother verifies that he did. Ralph doesn't recall ever punishing his children physically, but he believes his wife. Ralph simply states, "I hope you can forgive me." Rita looks into his eyes and says, "I already have forgiven you, now you must forgive yourself."

"I will never be able to do that," Ralph says.

Rita knows forgiving oneself is a much harder task than

forgiving others. Forgiving oneself and recognizing that one has betrayed the Truth of one's own being is one of the most painful things to feel.

Rita knows that holding onto things, especially negative emotions, blocks a person from awakening the dream that is within the depths of their heart.

# Truth

Truth is deep, it is revealing.

To know it is a lifelong journey,
A purposeful movement toward
The center and then out again.

Truth is illuminating, shimmering light
That enters into all moments when it is quested
It will not seek you out.

It is our desire for Truth that brings us to it.

The light of Truth Unifies with its shadow
And they become One.

As a teenager, Rita sets a goal to see the world by the time she's forty. Traveling makes Rita feel alive and connected to the world. Whenever there is an opportunity to see and experience something new and different Rita gravitates towards it. Rita feels that the more a person opens up to new experiences, the more open they are to knowing themselves.

Rita's parents have divorced, changing the structure of their family and the patterns between the feminine and masculine forces that unite people in marriage. Rita feels grateful since she finds her father to be oppressive and malicious. Freedom from his domination is a relief to the inner Spirit gathering force and wisdom within Rita's body and mind. Rita begins to become aware of who she is without the controlling forces of her family. Rita excels in chemistry, physics and biology, as well as some of the liberal arts. Rita finds classmates who are intelligent and unusual and she feels comfortable in their midst. Rita observes her classmates and finds a rhythm that holds her own unique beat. She mingles harmoniously with their individuation.

When choosing a university, Rita looks for a setting away from the city atmosphere, a place nurtured by a natural environment. She finds this in Northern California and leaves home at seventeen.

During the summer before leaving for college, Rita takes a summer job as a camp counselor for the Crippled Children's Society. Rita's soul yearns to touch all aspects of humanity, even those that her mind and senses find unpleasant.

The camp is nestled in a forest of oak and eucalyptus trees. As the sun warms the bark of the trees, their scent fills Rita's nostrils with a delicious aroma, bringing peace to her mind and body. Rita loves the way nature is able to mingle with her body and mind so easily.

Rita takes a moment as she walks from her Volkswagen Bug to the orientation cabin to allow the sun to penetrate her tan skin. She feels it reaching into her bones, warming them from the inside out. The camp counselor job is a perfect bridge between high school and college for Rita. She meets interesting people and finds out how much she enjoys being with all sorts of different personalities. Her favorite week is with the mentally disabled campers. The campers and staff put on a talent show that allows full expression of their unique selves. Rita loves the unlimited expression of Jeremy, one of the campers, when he sings, "You ain't nothin' but a hound dog" in his cowboy hat, jeans, and boots, pretending to strum a guitar. He struts in front of the audience and belts out the lyrics. He gets a standing ovation and bows to the audience. Rita enjoys the freedom and support from everyone working at the camp.

Packing for college is simple. Everything fits into the blue Volkswagen Rita has owned since she was sixteen. Rita arrives at her dorm room to meet her roommate. Claire is a young woman with dark brown, shoulder-length hair. She's from Los Angeles. She is into fashion, movie stars, and is obsessed with her weight. Claire refers to herself as a "JAP," a Jewish American Princess, a term Rita is not yet familiar with. They were thrown together in a dorm lottery. Living in the rainy Pacific Northwest is a different reality for Claire, but she is up for the adventure.

First thing Rita does is move her mattress off the bed frame and onto the floor where she feels more comfortable. She and Claire arrange their dorm room with personal effects representing what is important to them. Rita has driftwood, shells, and peacock feathers by her bed. Claire has pictures of her family and trinkets spread along her shelf.

What they have in common is their differences, and they both enjoy and languish in these differences. They both experienced their parent's divorces at similar ages and occasionally enjoy sharing their feelings around this topic. Claire is deeply rooted in her Jewish heritage and Rita enjoys learning about traditions. Claire shares Jewish rituals and stories with her. Music, language, and ritual are always enriching parts of humanity, if they don't cause separation.

Claire and Rita decide to travel to New Zealand and Australia after their first year at university together. They spend the first part of their trip in New Zealand. They plan to get a bus pass, but relinquish the idea after talking with the travel bureau. Hitchhiking is an adventure in itself, for they never know who is going to give them a ride or where they will end up. Their travels bring them in contact with a wide range of characters as they travel the north and south Islands. The uniqueness of each encounter amazes Rita. She loves the unknown and never knowing who she will meet—a wealthy yacht owner, a husband traveling home from a family birthday party. Most drivers are not only willing to give them a ride, but also to put them up for the night in their home as well. The generosity that people bestow upon them warms Rita's heart, renewing her deep love for humanity. Rita learns to stay present and open to the moment presenting itself and observes that such behavior feeds her heart and soul in a way that allows her to relax and trust in whatever comes next.

By the time Claire and Rita arrive in Australia, they are comfortable and open to adventure and this is what they both communicate to the world. People occasionally misunderstand their openness and their genuine innocence, but no harm ever comes to either of them. The world and its people respond to the genuine exchange of feelings on multiple levels.

Rita and Claire have train passes for Australia. The trains are subject to all the strikes that Aussies seem to impose upon the public. This is a natural occurrence "down under," but new to Claire and Rita. They had such good experiences hitchhiking in New Zealand that they make hitchhiking their backup plan when the trains stop running. Australia's culture is completely different from New Zealand's. Hitchhiking is actually outlawed in Queensland due to the numerous homicides that have occurred along trucking routes in desolate parts of the countryside. Claire and Rita decide to stay close to the train routes in Queensland.

On the way down the gold coast of Australia, the trains stop frequently all day and night. The train station for Brisbane is located just outside city limits in the middle of a sugarcane field. Its scheduled stop is at midnight for passenger pick-ups. Rita and Claire leave the youth hostel and head for the train station. The weather is warm and the night clear. Rita, loving the night sky, gazes up to the blackness in search of familiar constellations. They are wearing their backpacks as they walk alongside the train tracks. No lights and no other people are visible. Rita and Claire are alert to their environment as they pass through hulking shadows made by the sugarcane refinery. Something in the air makes the hair on their arms stand at attention. Their eyes have adjusted to the darkness and all their senses are keenly attuned.

As they round the bend, they see the little train station at the same time they hear the sound of a car. The car slows as it gets close to them and Rita can see it is full of young aboriginal men. One of the young men opens the window and leans out. He smells of beer. "You want a ride?"

"No thanks," Rita says. "We're catching the train just up ahead at the station, but thanks for the offer."

The car takes off and Rita turns to Claire. "Walk as fast as you can to the train station. I don't like how this feels, my heart is pounding."

The car turns back around at the same time Claire and Rita reach the station. This is fortuitous. They step inside where there is only one little old man. Without thinking, as if possessed, Rita drops her pack and walks outside. As she rounds the corner of the building, she sees that one of the young men is heading towards her. She looks straight into his eyes. "Thank you for making sure we got to the station safely. They are waiting for us inside and the train will be here any moment."

The young man looks at Rita, but remains silent, as if stunned by what she has just said. The man just stands there with his mouth open. No words come out. Rita turns and walks back into the stationhouse and the young man stares at Rita's back, wondering what just happened. The train comes and Claire and Rita get on it, feeling grateful for their safety as they nestle into their seats.

"God, that was a close one," Claire says. "The whole thing makes my stomach tight. Rita, do you think they were going to harm us?"

"I'm not sure, but I didn't think about what I was doing," says Rita. "I was just listening to something inside and responding to the moment. I had no thought about what and why I was doing what I was doing."

"It was like you were possessed," Claire says, "and I was caught up in the swell of energy that was moving around you, too."

They are silent with each other, both acknowledging the presence of some unseen force and partaking in an experience that goes beyond the boundaries of Rita and Claire. Sometimes things like this happen and Rita thinks about the incidence after it occurs, wondering what was guiding her to handle the situation as she had. She knows deep down that something different is created with the use of a few well-chosen words and the ability to be present and deeply rooted in the moment. Rita observes that one can change an outcome by meeting the situation with a different energy and thought, creating something outside of an existing belief and pattern. This is something that comes easily and naturally to Rita. Even if she doesn't understand it, she often witnesses its power and magic.

# Judgment

The dividing force between

Right and wrong,
Black and white
Masculine and Feminine

Inside and outside
Shadow and light
Heaven and Earth

Who sits in the place that divides?

It must be the mind of man, dividing so many things.

Young adulthood is filled with exploration on many levels for Rita. The sexual energy that accompanies these strong forces brings up many experiences for her. How these bodily sensations and urges intermix with the feelings within her heart become a focus. Even during childhood, sensations and arousal are present within Rita's little body, but nothing like they become in adolescence and adulthood.

During high school, she channels these feelings into her head and uses them for academic success. But in college, they overpower her. Rita's body vibrates with sensation and she uses her muscles to control them. Deep within the tissues of her sensate body she knows it is not safe to have these energies be visible in the physical world.

These are not conscious feelings but feelings Rita discovers as she enters the realm of sexual intimacy with men. The differences between men and women are not obvious growing up, but as she develops into a woman they become more and more visible in the world.

Rita finds her surges of sexual feeling both unsettling and pleasurable. The tension that comes with this conflict carries a fearful excitement she cannot control. Rita wants the pleasurable experience without the fearful component. Rita is physically attractive with long, brown, curly hair. She is athletic. Her skin is tan. She has brown eyes. Intensity and warmth emanate from her. All this is attractive to men. In the beginning, Rita lets her ego have this energy and finds her sexuality has a power over men. This allows Rita to have sexual experiences with men without feeling afraid. It creates a palpable distance between her and the other.

When she has these experiences with men, she doesn't recognize the distance and separation. All she knows is that the pleasurable part of sex is not reaching her heart the way she longs it to. Rita has relationships with men of all types, with different looks, different personalities, but none cross the invisible barrier to her heart. Actually, it is her body that yearns to be met in such an intimate way, where she can lose all control and merge into nothingness.

She eventually meets a man named Chris with whom she feels she can learn how to love with her entire being. She feels he will not intentionally hurt her. There is a pureness about Chris that puts Rita's ego structure behind her instead of in front, allowing a more intimate connection.

Chris is over six feet tall with a slender, athletic build and blond wavy hair, keen blue eyes, and a nice smile. He is quiet and unaware of his good looks. He has an angelic quality that Rita is drawn to. Being in her "power mode with her sexuality," Rita asks Chris out on a date after meeting him at a friend's potluck.

Chris is a good kisser and Rita feels his mouth could swallow her whole. The first date puts Rita at ease. Chris's easy-going nature allows Rita the chance to feel her heart in his company without a struggle. She is grateful for this and the relationship begins in a natural way during Rita's junior and senior years at college.

Observation is something that comes naturally for Rita, but she recognizes that opinions and judgments flavor her experience. This awareness is subtle, and the ability to witness how her mind works takes years of focus. Right after college, Rita begins the meditative practice of stilling her mind. She becomes aware of something within pulling her, nudging her, but it's nothing she can see or put her finger on. But it occurs as she is able to quiet her mind and listen in the silence. Meditation is a discipline and Rita's upbringing has encouraged discipline, so it's easy for her to add time for meditation during her day.

Rita seeks moments of silence whenever she can. She recognizes that being out in nature, whether digging in the garden or hiking a mountain, allows her to connect with this invisible part of herself. The solitude of the dirt and natural sounds of water, birds chirping, and wind whistling quiets her mind, slows her thoughts and allows something else within her to awaken. These subtle realizations help direct Rita in her life. Chris's quiet nature lends to sharing time in the solitude of nature. A sense of connection happens in the silence of their time together, weaving invisible threads of light together.

Most of the time, Rita feels as though she is blind, reading the world as if by Braille, feeling and fumbling her way through life. At first, the fumbling is awkward and she is self-conscious, but after a while she becomes comfortable with being uncomfortable. Sometimes, Rita finds herself fighting all conformities that make most people comfortable, forcing others out of their comfort zone. This unnerves many people. As Rita develops her ability to stand firmly on the ground, it proves to serve the invisible source that is within. No books instruct her. She pays attention to that which is occurring around her and what she is sensing, and that is what helps guide her.

Rita finds herself in unusual circumstances. She is called to something in the physical world that doesn't make sense. She begins working with the criminally insane in one of the largest forensic hospitals on the West Coast. The hospital is an all-male facility, built in the 1960s. In the old days, the hospital was fully self-contained; it even had its own surgical suite. Once a person was placed inside a facility like this by the courts, they were not released until they were no longer considered a danger to themselves or others.

This particular state hospital is home to about one thousand men. The entire facility is concrete with three-story high walls on each of the two main wings. The walls serve as barriers to the outside world. Dimly lit, windowless corridors lead to individual units that house the men. Each unit holds roughly twenty-five men living in individual rooms, individual cells.

Rita is unsure what draws her into such a dark part of humanity. She trusts there is a reason even if it is unknown to her at this time. Somewhere deep inside, Rita recognizes that even these shadowy, distasteful and malevolent parts of humanity are part of the whole. She feels it is important not to fear them. Rather, she tries to understand them. Society judges these aspects of humanity by locking them away, pretending they are not part of the whole.

Entering the institution, Rita first notices the change in the air. It is no longer fresh and lit with sunlight, but has a staleness, as if life barely exists within the molecules themselves. She feels as though she is entering a darkened cave where light does not reach. Once her eyes adjust to the dimness, she walks through a metal detector and lays her backpack on a conveyer belt to be x-rayed for contraband. A buzzer sounds and Rita moves into a "sally port" where her face and badge are scrutinized, identifying her as someone allowed to enter the long gray hallways that echo and smell of tobacco and sweat.

The men living within these walls were sentenced there by the court system after committing crimes against society. Rita is fascinated with the human mind and she is both disgusted and magnetized by reading the histories of the men she works with. She reads about Marshall Clyde, a short, stocky black man who always smiles and says, 'Hello' to Rita as she enters the ward. Marshall has worn the heels down on his black patent leather shoes due to a constant rocking motion, a side effect of Prolixin, an antipsychotic. He was brought up in New York City and his parents locked him outside in the middle of winter as punishment when he misbehaved. He was forced to sleep in a cardboard box on the city's streets. God only knows what happens to eleven-year-old boys sleeping on the streets of New York City. Marshall's crime was hideous—while high on crack cocaine he killed his girlfriend and cut her into little pieces. Since his arrest, he has been housed within these walls.

Rita allows herself to meet Marshall as he is in this moment. He opens the door for her, smiles, and she returns the same courteous behavior. At first, Rita feels strange. She's a young woman working in a locked facility with all these men. Other women work within the walls, but Rita feels surrounded by only men. She recognizes that if she treats these men with respect and honesty, then that is what she receives from them. This is not the case with all the inmates. In most of the men she sees, she can recognize a human heart, even if it is covered by many years of debris and neglect. When she finds that part of them, she concentrates on the spark of light within them, even if it is only a flicker. This almost always brings out their best and allows Rita to feel safer among the male population. Occasionally, she comes across an inmate who has no visible light. These men she tries to avoid, for they threaten her in a profound way. Her hair stands at attention when their cold, hard, deep, penetrating stare is directed her way. Rita feels their piercing eyes looking for a way to harm or manipulate the light within her. They seem to have a passion for taking light and fracturing it into pieces, so that it becomes unrecognizable from its origin.

When people allow real connection to occur, even fractured connection, she observes that they are much less likely to act out than if no connection is made. These observations are both conscious and unconscious for Rita. They help her recognize that all human beings have the potential to act either way, yielding destructive outcomes that harm themselves or others, or constructive outcomes that create something positive.

The five years Rita spends within these walls allow her to know at a very deep level that even in the darkest part of a human being there is almost always a spark of light. This spark can light the way, illuminating a journey back into relationship. This knowledge helps Rita hold out a light for humanity even when she is burdened by the world's daily negativity.

Rita works with this hospital population until she is able

to carry the light and is no longer separate from or fearful of this part of humanity. Most separation stems from fear created by the mind that judges itself as separate from something it is experiencing, or not wanting to experience.

# Masculine

The left brain
Half of the whole

Out of balance
Lacking insight
Separating from wholeness.

My passion is logic
Incessant thought drives me
My quest is to solve problems
My limitation is to see only part of the solution.

No longer relating to the living
Finding myself empty
Longing for the other half
That has been abandoned long ago.

Stretching herself beyond limitations is part of Rita's nature. This can be seen as she challenges herself to run a marathon, or make choices that lead her out of her comfort zone. These choices are instinctual for Rita; she finds that whenever life becomes too comfortable, too static, something starts to harden inside and Rita feels less connected to life.

Rita observes that in nature everything changes constantly—night into day, weather patterns, seasons, the daily temperature fluctuations. The web of life is dynamic. She sees human beings shying away from change, finding comfort in the status quo. The less change people are confronted with, the more comfortable they seem to feel. How could the freshness of everyday life be so threatening to most people? Rita contemplates this dilemma throughout her life.

Rita eventually marries Chris, the man she met in college. They find a way to be together harmoniously, yet continue their own unique individuation. This is rare, Rita observes in couples her age. She feels the expansion within her chest when she thinks of Chris, rather than a relationship that limits the vastness of her heart. This relationship assists in expanding Rita's heart and her ability to love—men especially—with her body.

Chris is constantly challenged by this dynamic flow of life that moves through Rita—sometimes like a wildfire and sometimes like a small stream of water. In the beginning of the relationship, Chris felt unbalanced by Rita's need for change. But as he realizes it has nothing to do with him, he relaxes in the ebb and flow of her dynamism.

Chris loves the natural world, too, and engages in many activities that cause him to interact with its dynamic power. He is an avid waterman, relishing ocean sports like surfing, wind surfing, and kite boarding. He learns to interact harmoniously with the powerful forces of nature found in the wind and ocean. These sports are a way of life for Chris. He finds his activities quite spiritual, bringing him in touch with the wisdom of the earth and the forces of nature. In turn, they also help him interact with Rita in a harmonious and connected way, yielding to a wisdom that allows the love between them to grow strong and unified without being limited to the constructs of traditional marriage.

Rita feels pulled to work overseas, but finds herself conflicted about leaving her marriage for an extended period. She'd be gone months, perhaps a year. Rita brings up the subject to Chris several times. "Chris, I feel an inner need to volunteer overseas. I feel a pull to stay here with you and a pull to go. I haven't been able to get clear on the two directions."

Chris finishes chewing his mouthful of food and looks over at Rita. "Rita, I can tell this is something you need to do. You've been talking about it and I think you should do it."

Something in Rita's chest relaxes as she takes the next breath in. "I didn't think I needed your permission to go, but I guess I wanted your blessing and the support of love that is within our relationship."

Rita goes over to Chris and motions for him to move out from the table so she can sit on his lap. Rita sits down and presses her body tight up against his, kissing him tenderly and caressing his neck. Chris's selfless giving comes from a deep wisdom within him, igniting the love within Rita's heart and causing an invisible flow to move between them. It could have been felt by anyone standing near them. Their kind of love is dynamic and flowing, built on trust. It doesn't match society's current image of marriage.

Rita is confronted with, "What do you want to do that for?" from her family. "Aren't you worried that Chris will find someone else while you are gone?" and "How could you leave him for that long?" are statements from co-workers.

"If I were worried," replies Rita, "I wouldn't be going. I have no control over what someone else does or doesn't do." Rita and Chris are not dependent on one another. This allows room for other experiences to occur.

In the beginning of their relationship, Rita and Chris have needs they want fulfilled. Most relationships form in the hopes that the partner will fill needs left over from childhood. Such relationships, based on unfulfilled needs recreated in adulthood, are obviously and unconsciously different experiences. Unfortunately, until one becomes conscious of this, the person continues to recreate similar relationships with dependencies that can be mistaken for love. Chris and Rita realize that one needs to fulfill one's own needs in order to be free to love. This firm inner ground is what allows the depth of trust and intimacy to grow between them, nurturing their union.

Rita begins an investigation of international agencies, looking for one that upholds the values she lives by. She selects one and starts the lengthy application process that includes an interview in New York City. Rita settles on a flight to the city, spending the night in the city, participating in the interview, and flying back home the same day. It is one of those quick decisions where the plans easily fall together. But, as happens many times, things don't go as planned; they go as they are meant to go.

Rita has a plane change in Denver but the Denver plane is unable to take off due to technical difficulties. No hotels are available because of a convention happening in town. All of the plane's passengers cue up in front of the service counter. Rita stands next to a businessman who lives in New York City. He is on the phone with his wife, who is looking for a flight into the city on her computer. The man is middle-aged with short, brown, curly hair, a medium build, and appears friendly. He relays the flight information to Rita. "There is a red-eye that gets you into the city tomorrow morning on Jet Blue."

Rita calls the airline, finding an even better flight into the city. The businessman overhears the details as Rita speaks into her phone. "Can I talk with the agent?" he says.

Rita hands her phone to Anthony, the name of the businessman. Then the phone gets passed down the line to the next four passengers in order to avoid the twenty-minute hold. They all get tickets on the same flight.

Rita originally plans to land in a different airport. She worries about finding the airbus and getting to her hotel to shower and change in time for her interview at 10 o'clock the next morning.

"Will you direct me to the airbus when we land in New York?" Rita asks Anthony. "It's a different airport than I had originally planned."

"No problem," he says. "When we land in New York, I'll

give you directions."

Rita calls her hotel. "Hi, my name is Rita Lovely. I have a booking for tonight but I am stuck in Denver and won't arrive until morning. I would still like to shower and change clothes before my interview."

"Fine," says the receptionist. "We'll see you when you get in."

Rita boards her new flight and dozes off for a brief sleep. She feels encouraged by how life finds a way to work itself out.

The plane lands and Rita looks for Anthony. Rita smiles at him through her bloodshot eyes. "Can you point me in the direction of the airbus?"

Anthony returns the smile. "I can do better than that. I can give you a lift into the city."

"Great!" Rita feels as though the universe is taking care of her as she walks beside Anthony. They leave the airport together and are greeted by a limousine driver who takes their bags and loads them into the trunk.

"Where are we dropping you?" the limo driver asks.

Rita reads off the address of the hotel to the driver.

"I know where that is. It's uptown."

During the drive, Rita learns about Anthony's wife, his children, and his work. He is obviously proud of them because as he speaks, Rita feels his heart shining. Anthony also has a sister, a physician, who started a clinic in Belize. He gives Rita a contact number for her in case things don't work out in the interview. They arrive at Rita's hotel and Rita gives Anthony a thank-you hug. The hotel receptionist welcomes Rita, giving her a key to room 105 at no charge.

They hold her luggage behind the counter and Rita walks to her interview, arriving fresh, energized, and on time.

What mystical breath is aligning these events, Rita ponders as she walks to her interview.

Sitting in the outer office of the international agency, Rita can't help but feel awe by life's perfection. The trip unfolds in a sequence that could never be planned, yet is so absolutely perfect. Her heart is filled with gratitude as she enters the interview. Later that day, Rita flies out of New York, physically exhausted but internally inspired by life.

It takes several months, paperwork, and a few more phone interviews before Rita is off to Uganda, Africa, to work in an HIV/TB program. Rita has worked in Public Health for a number of years, focusing on communicable diseases and HIV, which prepares her for whatever she might experience overseas. HIV and TB are quite different in Sub-Saharan Africa from what is common in the United States.

Rita trusts the invisible current that runs through her life as it unfolds moment to moment. Over the years, she has learned to shed the concepts and views that others hold, by learning to listen to the mystery that contains wisdom deep within the heart.

Driving from Kampala to Arua gives Rita a taste of Uganda. Red dust billows up from the tires as the truck driver tries to avoid potholes. Rita feels open, like a child exploring a new room. Everything is unfamiliar to her senses. The new stimulations do not assault her senses; they draw her in like an invitation. 'Come experience me,' is what the landscape says to Rita as her eyes take in the *tookus*, brick huts with thatched roofs, plantations of *matokee* and fields of maize. People with ebony skin carry heavy loads on their heads as they walk along the roadways that lead to towns. Children smile and wave as we rattle by in our white vehicle with red letters.

Rita is assigned to work with a team that travels daily to various locations in the West Nile region of Uganda. Her team consists of a physician from Australia named Marc, a Ugandan counselor named Katende, and a driver that varies from week to week. Rita is the nurse and it is her role to supervise the team. The team's goals are to assist Ugandan healthcare workers in becoming safe and self-sufficient as they care for and treat patients with HIV. This is a difficult if not impossible task, coming from a western healthcare perspective. It cannot address the realities that Ugandans face every day. This "simple" task—to bring anti-retroviral therapy to assist in the treatment of HIV in a setting like Africa—is quite monumental.

Rita is conflicted by what she observes and feels. Simple tasks, such as ordering medication, are almost impossible for the Ugandan healthcare personnel. Infrastructures do not operate with any consistency. Telephones, computers, fax machines, and postal services are sporadic due to lack of money, lack of electricity, and the misuse of funds. Rita often wonders what were they thinking when they brought anti-retroviral medications here? Are we causing more harm than good by creating resistant strains of virus? Are we causing a disease process to worsen by intervening? Questions continued to surface in her mind at the end of her frustrating days.

Rita is exhausted from long drives on hot dirt roads,

dealing with one problem after another—including Ugandan healthcare personnel who resist the interference of Europeans (we need you, but we resent needing you). Their resistance flits in the background of all conversations.

Marc is a young physician in his early thirties. He was born in China but grew up in Australia. He has a quiet nature. He is methodical, athletic, and is a talented musician. Rita and Marc sit on the rooftop of their home, watching the sunset, listening to their neighbors speak their Lugbara language. They try to combine the goals of the organization with the realities they are confronting in Uganda. Marc has been in Africa for three months prior to Rita's arrival. Each time a new member of the team arrives, new ideas are implemented, which keeps things dynamic. Once Rita recognizes that her role is to assess what might best serve the people, she settles down to work.

Marc struggles because there is such a limited healthcare system in Africa. He learns to practice medicine in a different way. He cannot rely on expensive tests because there are none available. He must rely on basic medical practices between patient and doctor. His assessment and interview skills are what he learns to trust, rather than lab results. Rita enjoys working with both Marc and Katende, the Ugandan counselor. They get to know each other well during the long car rides. They find they share many of the same views.

"*Ningunee*," Rita says as she reaches out her hand to Katendee when he gets in the Land Cruiser. There are customary greetings and handshakes each morning. The driver today is Sylvester, their favorite. His brother is an emcee who creates cassette tapes that they listen to during their drives. Sylvester is also the most talented driver they have. He is trusted to maneuver out of awkward situations they encounter with other Africans. Tribal mentality is still prevalent in Sub-Saharan Africa and each area speaks a different language. Sylvester speaks all four of the languages they encounter, making him invaluable.

Halfway to their destination is always a bathroom break. Sylvester looks for a suitable area of privacy for both Rita and the men. They climb back in the vehicle, settling in for the remainder of the drive. Rita always asks for Katendee's opinion before trying something new. This is new for Katendee. Normally, the expats don't ever ask Africans for their opinions. Rita finds Katendee's opinions and thoughts crucial when attempting to solve problems.

Rita observes that teaching and learning are done very differently here from how they are done in the United States when she attends a class given by the Ugandan healthcare organization. She decides to ask other Ugandans to teach the people about vertical transmission of HIV (mother to fetus), rather than teach the classes herself. It takes a bit more effort, but it is empowering for the Ugandans to be so respected and her decision is received well at the surrounding clinics. Her plan is to support the Ugandans in learning to problem-solve for themselves, rather than appearing to be the white knight riding in on his white horse to save the day.

This is a very different stance to take and is not received with open arms by Rita's superiors. She has stumbled into the unconscious condescension that we, the

European physician and scientist, know more than the Africans do, and therefore we have all the answers. But the standard solutions come out of research in a lab and do not apply to the reality when serving in Africa.

Rita wonders how many times in all of history that man intended to help others but caused additional problems due to his shortsightedness and limited understanding of the full scope of the problem. Rita holds her ground in her position to empower the Africans so they can come up with their own solutions to problems. This, of course, is not received well by the Africans because they have gotten used to Europeans coming in, taking over, and rescuing them economically and from disease.

The main problem that Rita sees is that this method is not sustainable, especially with the growing numbers of Africans placed on new, more affordable anti-retroviral therapy. Rita and Marc are never able to come up with the complete solution while they are in Africa, but they do sprinkle a bit of new thought into a pattern that is clearly not working. They can see both sides of the coin, but can find no easy solutions.

Rita's heart grows to hold all that she experienced. The suffering, injustice, pain and cruelty that seems to be everywhere is mixed with the African smile, the strength of the people, and their incredible joy that comes from music and dance. Rita observes that allowing a natural enfolding to occur gives the best results. This of course does not serve the business world, which looks for action and quick results in order to show profit. But in the end, what is the cost?

# Feminine

Hidden from view
Unknown to most
Forgotten like a lost art,

Steeped in wisdom
Graced with creation
Being called to awaken,

Out of touch with its partner
Remembering its real purpose
To unify with its other half.

**R**ita is comfortable with men. They are generally more direct and less hidden than women are. The only time this is untrue for Rita is when sexual feelings are involved. It is then that she finds men more secretive and less honest. Sexual feelings are powerful and not everyone is able to contain them or own them. For many, the surges of sexual feeling are split due to the force they exert upon the ego structure. There is also a general unease that society has with sexuality. Sex is either exploitive or sequestered, but not usually honest or open.

Women, on the other hand, are less direct, more hidden and secretive, but this is not how Rita tends to behave. Rita sometimes finds communication to be awkward when she deals with her same gender. More often than not, women are threatened by Rita. It is not until later in her life that Rita learns that it is her self-confidence and self-assurance that puts other women on the defense. When Rita stops to just observe women and how they hold their bodies, she becomes acutely aware of how many women are uncomfortable with themselves. Women tend to use their bodies as manipulative tools to get what they want from the opposite sex, or they are awkward with themselves. Athletes are a bit different because they learn to have a relationship with their bodies and use them for athletic endeavors. It is rare that Rita observes women who derive physical pleasure from being women who enjoy their own sensuality.

What strikes Rita the most is the lack of comfort women have with being themselves, or knowing what comfort with themselves is like. The role of women in Western society has changed greatly over the last few generations. Women are now in the workforce, competing for the same positions as men. Women approach situations so differently from the way men do. Women have learned to adapt to the ways that men approach problems, and have forgotten the innate wisdom they carry.

Women have a unique creative style when approaching problems, but most women have forgotten this because it isn't modeled to them as children. A lot of other things are modeled to girls as they watch TV shows, most of which do not exemplify the feminine aspect.

The feminine aspect was not modeled for Rita as a child. She was a tomboy and competed with her brother. Her strength comes from an inner place of knowing and she has learned to rely on it rather than on societal concepts of femininity. As years go by, Rita becomes more comfortable in expressing these aspects of the feminine.

Rita wants to hike the Grand Canyon from rim-to-rim, so during the September before her fortieth birthday she begins looking for a group making that journey. She finds an all-women's group led by a woman named Melanie who has hiked and boated the canyon for years. Melanie is steeped in geological and botanical knowledge of the canyon. Rita calls a week before the departure date.

"We only have one spot left," the voice at the other end of the phone lines says.

"Perfect," says Rita. "I'll take it, it must be meant for me."

Rita arranges to meet up with her friend Jan, who is

driving through that area of Arizona from Texas. They plan to have dinner together the night before the Grand Canyon group departs for the north rim. Rita has known Jan since they met in a class about body psychotherapy. Jan is in her sixties, a woman who also listens inwardly, and they make a point to enjoy time together whenever possible. Once again, the universe makes connections possible. One only needs to listen attentively to know what is being communicated.

Jan pulls up in her Toyota Four Runner outside of Rita's cabin. They embrace and find an overlook on the rim of the canyon to take in its awesome beauty. The expanse and beauty of the canyon is felt in both Jan's and Rita's hearts; they turn and smile at one another with the reflection of beauty in their eyes.

The next morning, Rita meets the women she will be with over the next five days. The group is small, just seven women, most of which have come by themselves. The women are from all over the country and range in age from thirty-five to sixty years old. Their guide, Melanie, is five-foot-two inches with dark brown hair, a British accent, and a sparkle twinkling in her blue eyes. She reviews all the gear the women are to carry and helps them reduce the weight of their packs. Everyone has to carry three liters of water down in the canyon, so excess gear needs to be left behind.

The common theme among the women is nature—their love for it and their need to deeply connect with it. Rita carries all her own gear, food, and water. The women are there to connect with the earth, so their pace is comfortable and Rita finds herself alone as she hikes. This allows for a deeper connection. Speaking engages another part of the mind, which gets in the way of communing with the spiritual nature of life.

The weather is warm and sunny in September. It usually doesn't get above ninety degrees. As they hike through narrow canyons, the women are in shade and their skin is grateful for the respite from the sun. A few days are spent hiking separately, then meeting up together for lunch and dinner. Conversation ebbs as they become absorbed in the beauty around them. Melanie points out edible plants and geological points of interest, focusing the group's attention on unique places of beauty.

Several days in the womb of the earth, surrounded by superb views, the scent of sage, swims in fresh water streams, and sleeping on the ground under the canvas of stars allows them to be in the moment, harmonizing with everything around them. As the group reaches Phantom Ranch, an agitated man approaches the group.

"There was a terrorist attack on the Twin Towers two days ago!"

Rita listens but stays where she is, down in the womb of the earth, harmonizing in a state of Peace. That evening at camp, the group is rattled by the news and a couple of the women are clearly upset. The tranquil peace that softened their faces has turned to tight lines across their foreheads and tense muscles at their jaw lines. Rita listens to the women voicing their concerns, fears, and sadness for the terrorist attack of September 11. The catastrophe is clearly impacting a good portion of humanity above the rim of the canyon that currently separates the group from its chaos.

"We are here holding a State of Peace for the rest of

the world in this beautiful place," Rita says. "If we were supposed to be up there on the rim, then that is where we would be. But we are down here and we can send the message of Peace out to the world."

The women become silent hearing the truth of Rita's words. During the rest of the time they spend in the canyon, the women concentrate on the beauty and peace that is all around them. Once out of the canyon and back on the south rim, it is clear to Rita that something very big has happened. There are no other tourists around. All the shops are closed. Not one tour bus can be seen. It seems that this event has had a tremendous impact on humanity. The heart of humanity has pulled together all over the world, reminding people that we are all connected. Rita wonders why it takes a crisis to witness this unity when she always feels it within her heart. The prayers that come out of this crisis circle the globe. Slowly they become silent once again, the divine presence only a background drumbeat.

# Forces

The crack of thunder
The whip of the wind
The crashing of a wave
The tremble of the earth

All are forces that are out of our control
They come upon us without warning

Pushing and forcing
Something to happen
Something to change

For most, these forces are only felt and experienced
They are never seen with external vision

They arise out of the dark
And flow into the light of form
These forces themselves are light, but cannot
Be understood until they reach into form.

There are many things in life that just happen. Sometimes we never fully understand their purpose or their complete impact. If a person is a seeker of TRUTH, they will continue to follow the thread of light that helps to bring meaning and understanding to events and feelings that occur in their life. This allows them to realize the full beauty of each and every awakened moment that is lived.

Rita begins to see the artistry behind her life in flashes that are sometimes like a blink and other times like a five-minute video projected in her mind. These moments are when her life becomes more light than matter, illuminating the grandeur of what it means to be human.

Rita and Chris always check out places that might make nice future residences. Rita has been studying Spanish, and so they decide to take a week together and explore Puerto Rico. Rita plans to stay an additional week in San Juan to attend a Spanish-immersion class. The two like to travel and spend time together. They live in a rainy environment, so many of their destinations are to warm, sunny locations. Chris always wants to get into the ocean and to ride new waves. He also loves the ocean and coastline. Warm temperatures, sunny skies, temperate ocean waters, and time off allow them to connect with themselves and each other in very intimate ways. They both feel nourished on a soul level when they take trips together, each time falling deeper in love and finding new ways to connect with one another.

It is spring break and San Juan is crowded with all the vacationing East Coast students and families. Rita and Chris head out of the city toward the southeast part of the island. They have reserved a few nights at a luxury beach resort. They both enjoy being in natural surroundings more than the noise and crowds of a city. The resort has a beautiful inner patio surrounded by the modest villa guest quarters with ceiling fans, and open-air decks with ocean views. There is a large pool that opens onto a white sand beach and the Atlantic Ocean. The first thing they do is change into swimsuits and head for the surf. Barefoot, they explore the beach to the south and take a swim in the ocean.

Rita swims over to Chris and wraps her legs around him as he stands in chest-deep water. She loves to be close to him and kisses him softly. Her legs slide down to the sandy bottom and Chris presses his tongue into her mouth gently, exploring the cavity. Chris feels a throbbing and grabs Rita's hips and presses his pelvis against her. They feel the caress of the ocean rocking them back and forth. Rita reaches down to find his hardness and takes it firmly in her hand. Rita raises her eyebrows and says, "You want to try out the bed in our room?"

Chris just presses himself closer to her. He allows himself to relax and they walk hand-in-hand back to their room. They shower and slowly entwine in each other's energy, bodies and breath. When they can no longer tell themselves apart, a deep peace settles over them, filling the room with complete stillness. They continue to allow this depth of intimacy to soak deeply into their skin. This continues over the next few days, until their inner and outer movements are in harmony, with nothing out of synch. A new energy starts to pervade their relationship, which is neither Chris nor Rita.

Their week together ends faster than they want it to, but Rita looks forward to a week by herself in Puerto Rico. She has always nurtured an inner spiritual relationship with a source that she refers to as the Divine, Spirit, or occasionally as God. (She uses the latter the least since concepts cannot be applied to something she considers indefinable.) Rita observes within her own mind how judgments of any kind separate her from the experience of the moment. Her inner guidance has been trying to get her to experience the moment as it truly is without covering the present with anything that exists in her mind. She has been practicing this for years, but only recently is able to apply this wisdom to her experiences as they occur.

Rita intends to stay with each experience and feeling regardless of the thoughts that arise in her head. The first experience is with a taxi driver as she is driven from the hotel in San Juan to the apartment building where she will stay for the next week. The vehicle is a van and Rita is the only passenger. She decides to sit up front, next to the driver.

The driver is from the Dominican Republic. He is in his mid-forties, slightly overweight, with dark kinky hair, brown skin, and wears sunglasses that cover his eyes. He asks, "Where am I taking you?"

The air conditioner makes a hissing sound as the driver pulls away from the hotel. Rita reads the address to him. "I'll be staying with a Puerto Rican lady for the next week while I study Spanish. My husband and I just spent a week over in Punta Rincon."

"Oh! That's a pretty part of the island, but why your husbands want to leave you here alone?"

"He has to go back to work."

The driver nods and looks down at Rita's tan legs. "You have beautiful skin color," he says, running his tongue across his lips.

Rita feels his mind touching her leg and fears his hand will follow. She decides she does not want this type of interaction and pays attention to the tone of her voice, directing his attention back to himself. In a kind and smooth tone she says, "Have you always lived in Puerto Rico?"

The driver settles in his seat and tells Rita details about his life. There are no further uncomfortable interactions. The driver seems to enjoy his interaction with Rita and carries her bags to the gated apartment, where he leaves her without incident. Rita consciously remembers her intention to stay with the experience without separating through judgment, and continues to follow her intention throughout her stay in Puerto Rico.

Rita is aware how relaxed she feels, how connected she feels to what she is experiencing. She enjoys being present with her experiences and is conscious that it allows for magic to occur between people.

During her week in Puerto Rico, Rita meets a woman named Alice. Alice is a physician from Massachusetts who is studying Spanish in the same immersion program. They are immediately attracted to one another, and seek each other out during classroom breaks. Alice is younger than Rita; she is in her early thirties. Her husband will fly down after she completes her week of instruction. Alice is close to six feet tall, with fair skin, straight light brown hair, and a child-like appeal.

The two women share none of the usual nuances of new friendship. They experience an immediate ability to share intimate feelings with no fear of judgment or rejection. An easy connection, without all the normal barriers people erect, allows them to have real conversations with meaning. During dinner in San Juan, as they listen to Sade sing, Alice says to Rita, "I wrote in my journal last night how good it is to see you again."

Rita smiles. "I know we've been friends in previous lifetimes and I love seeing you again, too." Rita takes a deep breath and feels her heart acknowledge the love that exists between them.

Jackson, a man from Ghana who now lives in the United States, is also staying in the apartment with Rita. He is completing some schooling so he can sit for his optometry license. In the evenings they speak for short periods together. One evening, Jackson comes into the apartment clearly stressed, and says, "My blood pressure is two hundred over one hundred and my heart has been pounding as if it will jump out of my chest." Jackson knows Rita is a nurse and is confiding in her.

"What happened today?" Rita asks.

"I was studying with another student. We were practicing intake assessments when she took my blood pressure and heart rate. It was so high she drove me to the clinic near campus."

"Do you feel anxious or fearful?"

"Well, I have to pass this test. There are so many people depending on me."

"Jackson, I'm sure you will pass your test. You are doing

everything you need to. You may not want to pressure yourself quite so much. Do you think you had a panic attack?"

A serious stillness comes into Jackson's face and the tension there ebbs. His dark eyes soften. "Maybe," he said.

Rita allows the quiet to settle and embraces Jackson. He holds her so tight she can feel the arousal inside his jeans. Rita slowly pulls away, acknowledging him with her eyes. "You may want to reconnect with your wife on the phone," she says.

Jackson lets out his breath and softly says, "Yes." He smiles.

Rita is careful not to allow any further physical contact with Jackson until the morning she leaves for the airport and says goodbye to him with a hug. Jackson tenderly kisses Rita's cheek.

Rita practices her Spanish with the taxi driver as they head for the airport. She feels completely at ease as she checks in at the American Airlines desk. She makes her way to gate 4B and sits down at the far end of the waiting area so she can listen to Hawaiian music on her iPod and observe the other passengers. A favorite tune starts to play and her body moves unconsciously to the music. Her hips press to the right and then to the left against the hard plastic seat and her feet tap the tile floor.

Rita's eyes take in a Puerto Rican man in his mid-forties talking on his cell phone and wheeling his luggage behind him. His face looks inaccessible and his body moves mechanically to the row of seats in the center of the waiting area. The overhead speakers announce, "Flight 428 to New York is now boarding at gate 4B," and then the message repeats in Spanish. Rita boards the plane and finds her seat. She is traveling business class, using free air miles she has accumulated. Her aisle seat is in front, next to an emergency door, which provides extra legroom. She thinks, "This is the best seat I've ever had."

As Rita settles into her seat, a woman comes over and asks, "Would you mind switching seats with me so I can sit next to my husband?" She points to the man next to Rita.

"Where is your seat?"

The woman points to the middle row.

Taking a deep breath in and then exhaling, Rita says, "Sure, let me gather my things."

Rita thinks, "Easy come, easy go."

The plane is still boarding as she switches seats. Rita is placing her belongings under the seat in front of her when the Puerto Rican businessman she observed in the waiting area sits down next to her. She looks up and smiles, thinking, "This will be a boring flight."

Rita pulls out her journal and starts to recall events she wants to write down. Although this is a morning flight, a passenger is badgering the flight attendant for an alcoholic beverage.

"We do not serve drinks until after takeoff," the flight attendant says.

The passenger is complaining about the policy when the businessman next to Rita says, "People are so interesting to watch. That man just won't take no for an answer."

Rita acknowledges his comment, agreeing that people are quite unique and interesting. He introduces himself as Roberto and Rita introduces herself.

Roberto has black hair cut conservatively and combed back, a mustache covering his upper lip, dark brown eyes, and silver wire-rim glasses. He is of medium build, dressed in dark blue corduroy slacks and a striped shirt. Rita decides to engage in a conversation with Roberto. The conversation flows smoothly from one topic to the next.

"I work for one of the pharmaceutical companies here in Puerto Rico," Roberto says in a New Jersey accent.

The pilot interrupts to make an announcement. "We will have a delay of about an hour to repair the brakes. We ask you to remain boarded so we can take off as soon as the repairs are complete. The flight attendants will help those passengers with connecting flights." A woman's voice repeats the information in Spanish.

Rita looks at the time of her connecting flight from New York to Los Angles and says, "Looks like I won't be making that connection."

Roberto pulls out his handheld computer and starts to look for connecting flights. The flight attendant responds to the light Rita has pressed. "There will be staff to help you make new connecting flights once you arrive in New York."

"Thanks," says Rita and settles into her seat, relaxed, knowing there is nothing to be done right now.

During further conversation, Rita and Roberto discover they are a year apart in age and have been married for the same amount of time. Roberto asks, "Where did you go while you were in Puerto Rico?"

Rita describes her vacation in loving detail, as she can still taste each experience and feel the pleasure in her body as she recounts her trip. Roberto listens intently and Rita asks, "How many years have you lived in Puerto Rico?"

"We have been here the last five years."

"Do you like living here?"

Their conversation continues to flow and Rita asks, "Do you love your wife?"

"I don't know," Roberto answers.

Rita doesn't understand the answer but doesn't ask any more questions about his wife. She feels something under the surface of his skin that implies feelings of sadness, anger, and love all at once.

"Do you love your husband?" Roberto asks.

Rita feels a swell of love flow to the surface of her heart as she responds, "Yes."

Roberto speaks cautiously about his family as if he is protecting them from something, shielding them from a world outside the intimacy of family. As he relays information, Rita feels no warmth or depth of feeling, only words communicating information. At first, Rita doesn't notice anything special happening between herself and Roberto. She commonly has these types of connections with people, intimate yet maintaining separation on the physical level. Early in life, Rita experienced the deeper connection with people, but has always felt a sense of separation through the physical form, her body.

Roberto places his hand on Rita's arm as they talk and look into each other's eyes, and something starts to melt. Some invisible barrier that has always existed for Rita between the world inside and the world outside falls away. Every one of her senses is available to experience this moment, and she is observing and feeling at the same time.

Something starts to take over and she does not want to control it or stop it. She is curious and wants only to allow the experience. Roberto feels something flowing through him as well. He feels himself connecting directly with Rita.

The plane is now repaired and has finally taken off. The forces that have drawn Rita and Roberto together become stronger, eliminating any sense of separation. Roberto gives Rita his iPod and she listens to "Ave Maria" playing through the earphones. The song is one of her all-time favorite compositions. It is all she can do to keep herself composed and in her seat. Physical touch becomes more intimate as Roberto touches the palm of Rita's hand and she feels him enter her through the center point. He is exploring every part of her through this tiny point in her palm. He looks down at Rita's soft, full lips and parts them with his tongue. With the gentlest touch, he presses his lips to hers. Her body responds to his touch and she feels the sexual edge of what is transpiring between them.

She says, "I don't want this to be sexual."

Rita feels moisture building between the folds of butter-soft skin in her genitals.

"I am communicating directly to your body, exploring each and every part of you," Roberto says. "And I am feeling the response of your body inside of me." His touch and her body are one sensuous flow without any separation and with minimal physical contact. Rita's mind is no longer functioning in its usual capacity.

The normal physical boundaries around them on the plane also become softer and are part of what is occurring. This intimate form of communication/communion continues until they arrive in New York. It is as if they are the only two on the plane and everyone else is part of their experience.

"This is something spiritual, separate from our already existing lives," Roberto says.

Rita disagrees with him. "I do not see or experience physical reality as separate from spiritual reality. For me, they are One. That is what I just experienced with you."

Roberto does not respond. For him they are separate.

Once inside the terminal, Rita rebooks on the next available flight to Los Angles. She experiences soft edges around everything, as if the masses of people in the airport are ONE without distinct edges, and she is part of this whole. The connection between Rita and Roberto continues in the airport. Her body and heart completely give over to the experience. She is no longer in her head thinking; she is only the experience and the witness to it. She finds herself sitting in Roberto's lap, breathing him in, touching her face against his, letting her lips meet his, softly exploring him. Rita has absolutely no thought separating her from the experience and Roberto and Rita find themselves in a state of Oneness. Roberto has a direct experience of Oneness, but does not hold its consciousness.

Their breathing becomes synchronized, their hearts become one beat between them, and their two bodies are experienced as one. One complete experience, flowing in and out with each breath. Relating to each other as one instead of two.

"I feel completely at peace and completely content in this moment," Roberto says.

Rita just presses her cheek against his face. The time

continues forward and Rita hears the announcement that her flight is now boarding. She says good-bye to Roberto and enters the plane, continuing to experience the presence of Oneness. This flow and experience stays with Rita. It is as if the experience carries her forward, flows through her, and now she is a part of it consciously. Roberto's parting words are, "I know I'll see you again."

Roberto and Rita have exchanged phone numbers and e-mail addresses. It is hard for Rita to consider what all this means because it does not fit with anything she has previously experienced—at least not this kind of depth shared with another person.

Rita spends the night in Los Angles with her mother-in-law, Emma, who is quite ill. When Rita arrives home she tells Chris about her experience with Roberto. "I had the most loving experience with a complete stranger on the plane," she says.

"I think that is the way it's supposed to be with everyone," Chris replies.

Rita breathes in her husband and feels his truthful wisdom and the experience she has had with Roberto at the same time, pondering the consciousness of Oneness through her senses.

# The Invitation to Love

The air is soft and sweet
Like the breath of the Lover

Covering every inch of skin
Inhaling, tasting and savoring
The delicateness of the moment

Passion starts to build
Like a flame that turns into a fire

The fire starts to melt all boundaries
And the two become One
Moving in a rhythmic pulsation
Glowing from the inside

The light becomes visible in their skin
And in the air itself.

A poem arrives shortly after Rita returns home. It validates her experiences and some of her feelings, strengthening the connection between her inner and the outer. It also floats many questions to the surface of Rita's mind. Rita's heart is open and it doesn't have difficulty loving. The loving heart does not divide things or people; it unifies them. It feels natural to love both Chris and Roberto. The entire experience feels right to Rita's heart. It is her mind that doesn't understand things.

The force of energy that Rita experiences is strong, energizing, magnetizing, and unifying. Rita's head and thoughts are not in alignment with her heart, for the mind contains many structures and forms that do not allow unification with the physical world. Rita is unaware that she has embarked on a mystical journey that started prior to this embodied form and will continue for years after .meeting Roberto. The force of energy that has brought them together is strong and full of transformative burning heat.

"Rita, I knew you were going to call. I just needed to get to my office so I could answer the phone. Now it feels like a heater is next to me, radiating heat throughout my office." Roberto inhales deeply. "I wish you were here next to me."

Rita feels a powerful surge of energy inside her abdomen moving up into her heart. She feels an expansion in her heart and a happiness just from making telephone contact with Roberto. "I have a meeting in five minutes," Rita says as she takes a deep breath and says, "Goodbye."

"I love what love does," Roberto breathes out.

The phone clicks in Rita's ear, leaving a silence that

extends over thousands of miles.

These powerful forces are rarely experienced by human beings in such intimate ways. This kind of connection happened only once before for Rita, with a man she met five years ago. Rita was attending an international conference for body psychotherapists in California that lasted several days. During the conference, Rita felt someone staring at her and when she turned to her left she saw a man looking straight at her. He seemed to be trying to figure out something. Rita did not recognize the man with his salt and pepper hair, brown, sharp-lit eyes, and a thick compact body dressed all in black. She returned her attention to the front of the room.

The next day there was a workshop given by the staring man, whose name turned out to be Samuel. He said he was from Switzerland. During a demonstration, he took Rita's hand to illustrate a technique of breathing and moving with another person. Rita moved toward the man as he guided her forward with her right hand. He breathed in her essence as she exhaled. They had an immediate connection that Rita felt rise up the front of her body. Her body and mind recognized it as a powerful sexual exchange—one that vibrated through her body from the inside out. There was no personal exchange during the demonstration, just the dramatic awareness of feeling, both in her heart and in her genitals. Rita noticed her underwear was wet with excitement in response to this invisible current between the formless and form.

These bodily sensations continued throughout the conference, arousing all the dormant cells within Rita's body, causing her to respond willingly to this flow of energy. On the drive home, she could not contain the energy any longer, which made it hard to concentrate on driving. Rita drove her car off the road and massaged her genitals, relieving the muscle tension within her body. This allowed the powerful feeling to flow down her legs, connect to her feet, and then back into her pelvis and the rest of her body.

Rita has always enjoyed a rich sexual life and never feels deprived, but these feelings were different. Rita found herself responding to an invisible energy in a very visible way. It was pleasurable, but it was shared with an invisible force instead of another form. Samuel also felt the power of their connection and found Rita's phone number through the conference sponsors. He called her when he returned to Switzerland. Rita was surprised to hear from Samuel, but it was an externalized confirmation of what she had experienced.

Carrying all this sexual desire within her body, Rita felt that each cell was charged with energy to unify. Rita invited Chris to share in the energy.

Chris sensed something different, something more electric, and hungrier, as they found each other in bed. Chris enjoyed this new pleasurable flow and allowed himself to unite with it through his body. Rita allowed herself to be drawn deeper into her body with each orgasm. She began to connect with the deeper sexual energies that arose within her own physical body with less fear and yielding, less need to control. Rita found these energies not only pleasurable, but also nourishing to various feminine qualities arising within her consciousness.

Rita was drawn to continue her connection with

Samuel. They talked on the phone, sometimes with frequency and sometimes with long breaks, depending on the flow of energy between them. Samuel was a psychotherapist who worked with the body, so when Rita and Samuel communicated, there was a common language of understanding and insight. Samuel enjoyed talking with Rita; she was curious and open with how she felt. They explored this energy relationship with each other for several years, never seeing each other in person, only speaking on the phone and occasionally e-mailing.

Samuel experienced a divorce during this time and Rita spent six weeks in Spain. While in Spain, she contemplated going to see Samuel. By then, several years had passed and the sexual energy was not as strong. Rita experimented with the energy and shared it with Chris, which strengthened their physical connection and opened her heart more deeply, allowing sexual energy to flow into her heart. This allowed for a deep comfort and relationship with the powerful energy.

Rita called Samuel from Spain. Samuel said, "You could come see me in Switzerland. I won't touch you. It would be good to see you," said Samuel.

"You sound sad and in a lot of pain."

"Yes, the divorce is hard for me. I feel lost right now."

Rita just listened to Samuel's emotional state beneath his words. She sensed his vulnerability, his neediness and tremendous pain. In a soft quiet voice she said, "I feel it is better that I don't come see you right now. Instead, I will just send love and healing to you, Samuel. I'm sorry you are hurting right now. I'll call you when I get back to the U.S."

"Okay, Rita," Samuel said. "Thank you."

What was important was Rita's willingness to meet him and not be afraid of such a connection. Samuel was honest and open with Rita and this allowed them a unique friendship, accepting each other and loving each other without personal demands or restrictions.

When Rita returned home from Spain, she was clear about her relationship with Chris and her relationship with the world. She marveled at how much can change when being open and honest with oneself and others. The human heart, when open and willing to love, can change so much, yet when the heart is closed or unwilling to love, nothing can change. Everything becomes frozen in place, solid and immovable.

The connection with Samuel fulfilled its purpose and the sexual energy within Rita is now flowing much freer into the heart without fear binding it. Once or twice a year Samuel and Rita connect via e-mail or telephone but the energetic charge between them no longer exists; it flows freely—or at least in Rita. Having a partner like Chris is such a blessing to Rita, for he always says yes to love and allows a constant transformation to occur between them. This keeps their marriage vital with life-giving energies.

The energy that Rita experiences in her connection with Roberto is different. It relates to the heart as a deep longing. Their connection is one Rita's soul has longed for since the beginning of time itself. Rita's life and choices have brought her to this experience. Rita has meditated for twenty-five years and pursued spiritual growth as a central part of her life. Most of her choices flow from this place. Rita pictures

Roberto's life from the minimal amount of words they exchanged on the plane. Roberto lives the American dream. He has gone to college, met a woman, married, had two children, pursued his career, and made his career and family the central part of his life. This dream is deeply rooted in the collective consciousness of humanity in the United States. Rita envisions Roberto's conscious choices coming from values instilled by society, culture, family, and the business world.

The two of them are at opposite ends of the spectrum, although Rita has also gone to college and pursued a career and has family. However, what is central within her is her relationship to Divine Love—however that manifests itself.

Rita said to Roberto on the plane, "I've been preparing for this experience, a realization of what I know to be the Truth, for so long. How do you just get to have it?" Roberto smiled and just took in the experience and let it saturate each cell.

Rita rereads the poem that Roberto sent her with a photo of himself and the request that she send a photo to him. She re-experiences the energy, not wanting it to stop, as she thinks about sending a picture. She remembers a quote, "One never experiences divine love through the same form twice." Sitting with a photo of Roberto, she wonders if that is true as she e-mails a photo and a poem in return.

Roberto returns to Puerto Rico. He feels the effects of love and an open heart unburdened and abandoned. He calls Rita as he drives home. Chris answers the phone. "Just a minute," he says and hands the phone to Rita.

Roberto is open, ready to connect with Rita again, and it shocks him to have Chris answer the phone. His heart skips a beat and he jerks at the sound of Chris's voice. Roberto is irritated that he has intruded upon Rita's home, thinking he was calling a private line. The openness of his heart grows a slight membrane, constricting the flow of love. He hangs up soon after Rita comes on the line. She can feel his retreat as if an open window that easily let in the breeze or a breath of fresh air has suddenly closed. Rita experiences a sharp pain within her chest. She does not feel she is doing anything wrong. She thinks, "I am just being open, honest and loving. I am not trying to hide anything or change anything. That's why I gave Roberto my home phone number."

Chris already knows about Roberto, and more importantly, he knows what is in Rita's heart. Rita always feels honesty is the best policy no matter what. She also knows that not everyone feels the same way. However, it is what she practices. Rita senses what Roberto experiences. The feeling is strange and somewhat disorienting.

That first phone call starts a slow and painful breakdown of the most beautiful communion Rita has ever had, where the inner awareness and the outer experience become ONE. One constant and continual flow of creative awareness manifesting itself at the same moment it is felt within the human heart. Rita knows this is the deeper Truth of being human and one of the deepest potentials within the human heart. To lose it feels devastating. The wisdom within her heart is "Love No Matter What!" It is the essence of all that is in life, and it is the connecting force that unifies.

She hears these words like a mantra every time she feels the painful longing in her heart. "Love No Matter What," Rita tells Chris. "That was Roberto who called."

"What is he calling for? You know he only wants to have sex with you, which is just how men are."

Rita doesn't reply. She simply recognizes the deep split that exists in humanity between sexual feelings and heart-felt feelings, and allows this knowledge to sit in an open space. Rita goes to bed bringing her longing, which is like a deep ache in her chest. She breathes in and out, feeling the soreness and allowing the ache to be soothed by being present with the sensations. Rita and Chris make love as the swirling energies that have been brought to the surface by the phone call begin to connect with their bodies, their breath, and their conscious willingness to love. This helps to ground the forces of these energies into their relationship. Rather than causing a separation, it helps bring them closer together and allows Rita to have both experiences—that of separation with Roberto (physically), and that of unification with Chris.

These forces that can both unify and split are very powerful, and it takes a conscious effort for Rita to stay aware of their influences in her own inner self and the life she is living. These forces carry so much power coming up through the archetypical world, like a strong wind blowing through Rita and her life. They are powerful enough to both destroy and create through the human heart. It depends on the integrity of Rita and Chris as to what they will manifest in the physical world. Roberto has also been touched by these forces but is unprepared consciously and physically for their power, and in the moment they are manifesting in the first fragmentation of unity between human forms.

# Pursuing the Kiss

The kiss of the Divine,
So soft, so tender, so sweet, so warm
Covering the entire body

Waking up every cell
Returning all things into balance
Vibrating with life and creation

Something we wait an entire lifetime for
Bringing everything into ONE sensuous moment
Precious, BREATHING Life.

Something so new, so alive, is stirring in Rita every waking moment. Her feet don't touch the ground in the same way, food doesn't taste the same, and nothing seems to be the way it was before her encounter with Roberto. Somewhere inside she knows this has nothing to do with Roberto, but her ego wants to attach it to something so she can hold the experience and freeze it in time. This in itself illuminates a conflict between the Truth of the experience and the outer manifesting world.

The force of the experience upon Rita's physical body sends her conceptual mind into a state of chaos. The conceptual mind is made up of constructs easily seen in the physical world, bringing sense to what we see, feel, and experience. What Rita feels within her body and within the deeper resources of her heart does not fit with the surface understanding of her conceived sense of herself or the world. This experience and the sensations within her body are fluid, not solid. The awareness of herself as a form merging with the awareness of the outer world is no longer separate from what she is experiencing. The muscles and bones relax, becoming more open and flexible. There is acceleration in the flow of energy connecting to all of life through Rita's nervous system.

Rita comes from a family of scientists. Her father, Ralph, is a physicist; her mother has a degree in Biology. Ralph's two brothers both have Ph.D.s in chemistry and physics. This perspective firmly imprints certain viewpoints of the physical world upon Rita's brain. Because Rita always stays in connection with the natural world, observing and living close to it, she is constantly exposed to its fluid state. It is society and the interactions with the outer societal structures that do not support this fluid state; they support the need to keep a static conceptualized state in the world. It is this conflict that brings a sense of chaos into Rita's life. She cannot ignore the Truth of her experience with Roberto or what continues to arise as sensations in her body; they are more real, honest, and truthful than anything else.

Questions arise. Questions like, What does marriage mean to me? What is love between men and women? What is love that is unconditional and free to move? Concepts that the physical world sits upon seem to deny that Rita's experience of life is fluid. It is this fluid state of being that feels more real, closer to the breath of life. Initially, Rita feels so deeply connected to Roberto that it is as if they are one being. She is aware of what he is thinking and feeling even without contact in the physical world. She calls him often to validate this awareness, needing the physical world to make what she is feeling seem more real. Roberto still connects deeply within his own heart and he knows when Rita is going to call. Their inner connection continues and puts a magical glow around them, allowing them to maintain closeness across thousands of miles.

The flow of energy is like a river of water hitting against restrictions within Rita's psyche, which tries to remove them. The restrictions are perceived as painful at times. Rita is not new to this. She has worked at removing restrictions for many years on the physical, emotional, and mental levels of experience. These restrictions are anchors rooted deeply in the collective psyche of the world as well as within her personal psyche. This makes them very strong and working through them does not illuminate a noticeable flow or change in the outer world. It does allow more light to enter into Rita's awareness and illuminate more clearly the journey she is on.

Rita is now restricted to trusting the inner sensate world and her inner connection with Roberto, which guides her awareness. This restriction places an expectation upon Roberto to be there for Rita's unfolding process and to continue an open honest flow between them. Roberto has little within his own personal life to support such openness. The corporate world he spends most of his waking hours in does not support open honest relationships. In fact, he lives in a world where politics play out and hidden agendas exist on every front. It is also clear to Rita that Roberto is not open and honest with his wife. He never tells his wife about his encounters with Rita and keeps their interconnection secretive. Rita overlooks these things and continues forward, pursuing the flow of Divine Love. She pursues Roberto. She thinks and feels he is part of her quest for unifying with this energy. This activity within her own ego structure becomes increasingly problematic for Rita. The more she pursues Roberto, the more the flow between them dissipates. This creates a pain so deep and severe that it hurts Rita's heart. There are moments the longing is so great she wants to die rather than be separate from this Divine Love.

Rita is able to hold an awareness of objectivity, but the energy and the pain is subjective to her. She continues to move through the pain in a quest of unification with Divine Love. She hears the mantra, "Love No Matter What."

There are moments when Roberto frees himself and connects with Rita. But these are moments only and are not the constant flow Rita is questing. The connections with Roberto strengthen the energy flow in Rita, bringing deeper restrictions to the surface of Rita's awareness.

Roberto romanticizes their experience. "I have a new definition of love, Rita. Love isn't supposed to be painful."

Rita is aware of this immature concept of love and knows it is far from the Truth of Love. Love itself is bottomless and constantly seeks to unify with all of life. Rita knows love is the underlying thread that weaves life together and has nothing to do with pain. It is the separation of our awareness from this thread of love that causes pain. Rita is beginning to understand this separation within her awareness. It originates from all the internalized restrictions and the external structures that restrict the flow of love within that causes the pain.

Rita has an insatiable appetite to understand life and its nature and continues to seek out the mystery and the unknown that surrounds the experience she has with Roberto. At first, Rita understands that Roberto wants to explore this unknown together with her. This brings great joy to her, for it is not something Chris is interested in or able to experience with her. As time goes on, Rita learns that this is merely a projection that she places on Roberto and not a desire that he holds within his own heart.

Long ago, Rita realized that our outer lives are shaped by choices we make. It is this freedom of choice when it is known and exercised that can change most any experience. Along with choice comes responsibility for the situation.

Most human beings do not exercise this basic human power that was given to us at birth. Taking responsibility for our lives is not a standard for humanity. People tend to blame others and are unwilling to see the power of choice that exists within each situation. They are waiting for the outer world to change and determine who they are, rather than looking within to discover for themselves. This is a betrayal. Most humans living now experience the deep separation of the sensate and feeling world that lies within the body and earth.

Roberto moves further and further away from Rita in the outer world during their connections by phone and e-mail. He stops returning phone calls—says he will and then does not. Rita still feels the inner flow of love between them and does not understand the disconnection happening in the outer world. She hears the mantra, "Love No Matter What. Love." She follows this internal command when she feels pain searing in the center of her chest. Her mind tries to run away from the pain by offering explanations and questions. Maybe he is too busy to call back? Maybe he is out of town? The mind tries to split from the burning pain lodged between Rita's breasts, burning and heating her entire body and soul. Her eyes fill with tears and her body convulses into sobs. She wishes for death just to be relieved of this wrenching pain.

Somewhere inside, Rita knows this pain has nothing to do with Roberto. It is much deeper—reaching down into the soul and unveiling the essence of who she is. It is the split in Rita's awareness between the inside and outside world that is so painful. The simple truth of our essence—Love is not always easy to see or feel in the outer world. Rita begins to recognize that this pain covers most things in the outer world.

# Separation

I see you there swimming beneath the surface
Looking for a way out from within
Trapped under the crust of attachments made of ice
That separates the inner from the outer.

How does one break through?
With a fearless heart full of passion and love
Longing for the truth.

It takes time to melt the ice of the world.
Most are unaware of what lies beneath the surface
The journey is the remembrance of the fluid state
Between the outer and the inner.

The state of separation is an illusion that most live and few overcome
For the path takes determination and devotion to the truth
And a willingness to hold all things as ONE.

Rita continues to experience herself in new ways that change her experience in the physical world. One day while walking on the beach, Rita witnesses her body as completely transparent. Inhaling, the ocean seems to become part of her breath. Exhaling, she becomes part of the sky and sand beneath her feet. This total immersion with everything within the physical world becomes more frequent as days flow by. Rita longs to be able to share these experiences with others in the way she has with Roberto.

Rita and Chris begin to feel fewer restrictions within their bodies and their interactions with each other. Something within the cells of their bodies longs for the connection with the other. Neither Chris nor Rita questions this deep pull to merge with the other. There starts to be a current of "yes" to love, "yes" to life that becomes so loud and intoxicating that it drowns the "no" into the background of the collective mind and current restrictions within the physical world.

They experience this directly in their lovemaking. Instead of putting off these experiences or planning them in their heads, they both learn to listen to the flow moving within their bodies and to respond with their hearts and souls to love. As each touches the other's skin, an opening to a new experience begins. Their minds become absorbed in the moment and all thought is suspended. This allows a deep and real experience without the separating thoughts of the mind. As the flow progresses and the cells respond, their breaths become synchronized to the moment. As Chris moves so deeply within Rita, he is absorbed within her body and breath. Rita herself disappears into the moment and finds her body responding with passionate moans, pulling Chris closer and deeper. As the cells heat up, they begin to merge and vibrate with this new consciousness that flows from "yes" to "love," turning their hearts toward a deeper union with all of life.

Despite these beautiful connections with Chris, Rita continues to long for a physical connection with Roberto. She maintains an inner conversation with him and attempts to contact him regularly. Occasionally she catches him in a moment when he is not preoccupied with his job. He works long hours and has the title, "Director," which holds much power and responsibility. His connection with Rita is so unfamiliar in his everyday life that it has nowhere to fit. The connection is a puzzle piece with no space in the mural of his life. Roberto's life is filled with deadlines, meetings, business trips, agendas, e-mails, conferences, budgets, and efficient production. It is not filled with sensuous feelings, honesty, warmth, and organic flow. One has to be in the moment of an experience to connect with life. You cannot be planning the future or reminiscing about the past and feel the flow.

What was once tender, sweet, and intangible evolves into sexual feelings and talk that lacks the connection of love and all its warmth. When Roberto finds time to connect with Rita by phone, she feels a flow of sexual desire that reaches across thousands of miles into her body. Rita feels his every move, every desire upon her skin reaching deep into the recesses of her soul. Roberto enjoys the sexual feelings within his own body; they distract him from his business day and put him in touch with something more real within him. These interactions are always cut short due to poor cell phone reception or the demands of Roberto's corporate life. The resistance that exists within the physical world to the free flow of love becomes very tangible to Rita.

Rita finds herself frustrated after these interactions, for they never feel complete. Something is always missing between them and their bodies. An honesty develops when feelings are connected to their bodies, bringing about a more undefended state. These interactions begin to illuminate places within Rita that are not connecting to the flow of Oneness. They are easier to see in the interactions with Roberto than with Chris because there is no other physical person to become lost or enmeshed in. Rita's ego continues to project these feelings and beliefs onto Roberto, but they don't stick and Rita is left taking responsibility for them. It is her nature to share these revelations with Roberto, and she does, continuing to open herself to him and allow the light of illumination to flow into her body as she discovers these Truths.

Rita feels her heart expanding with love and picks up the phone without thought. She calls Roberto. The call interrupts a business meeting, interjecting a completely different vibration of energy into the meeting even though Roberto never answers the phone. Nevertheless, the connection between them is made. Rita reacts to the lack of response from Roberto with a mixture of feelings. Love is still available within her heart, but now there is frustration at not making the connection in the outside world. Rita becomes aware of deeper feelings of fear connecting with images of rejection from childhood. Rita's heart is still reciting the mantra, "Love No Matter What." This willingness of her heart to love brings more illumination and wisdom, filling the space between Puerto Rico and the West Coast.

The searing pain between Rita's breasts continues but lessens with time. The burning pain of separation starts to flake off the heart like charred paper, as love illuminates the deeper truth of the human experience. Rita still invites Roberto on the journey with her. She voices her feelings and projections, and owns them, so they are completely exposed to the light of day. This allows Rita to take complete responsibility for her experience rather than give it to Roberto, or blame him for it. This complete ownership allows transformation. Without ownership of an experience, nothing can be transformed. These interactions between Rita and Roberto continue for months, for years. As the "light of day" moves into Rita's experiences, she realizes that the pain is not about Roberto at all, but about her own sense of separation from the flow of energy, losing the awareness of love flowing both within her and around her.

The force of these feelings and sensations is great and continue to unfold. The illumination guides Rita into new and different experiences. Rita decides to attend a continuing education workshop for professionals in San Diego. She tries to find classes she is interested in, which would benefit her personally and professionally. This decision is last minute. She is not always sure why she is inwardly urged to do something, but knows it will be disclosed to her later and she trusts this process, for she has lived by it for years.

Rita is a nurse and a certified body psychotherapist. The class reviews anatomy of the mouth, neck, and head as well as how experiences can become lodged in the physical body, causing emotional and physical pain and repeating patterns within one's life. There are twenty-five students, an instructor and several teacher assistants to help guide the practical part of the class. The students work in groups of three for several days. Everyone receives work on his or her mouth, head, and neck. Rita has experienced mouth work in the past, but she now has all this energy moving through her body so the work seems to go much deeper.

The mouth and throat have to do with expression. It is also the segment of the body connecting the head with the heart. It is rare for someone to seek the Truth of their heart without analyzing and cutting off its natural flow. Currently, most of humanity lives through concepts and ideas within the head rather than in direct relation with life, thereby separating from their experience of life itself.

One evening after class, several students meet in the hotel bar to enjoy sushi and wine. They have interesting conversations. In particular, a woman named Tasha tells the group about her life in Russia. Tasha is in her late twenties, of medium height, with an attractive figure, fair skin and long auburn hair. Tasha's eyes are blue with a dull coldness that does not allow entrance or cast light onto her audience. Her voice, however, emits emotion as she speaks.

The group listens intently as she relays a story of being thrown into a car by a man outside of her apartment in her hometown. He blindfolds her, rapes her, and then throws her back onto the street from where she was taken. Tasha says, "Things for women became worse after communism fell and anarchy entered into our everyday lives."

"How did you get to the United States?" someone asks.

"I met my ex-husband through the Internet. He sponsored me to come to the US. The term is 'mail order bride.' Once he got me here I became his property, an object he owned. He locked me in his apartment when he went to work. But he never beat me. Eventually I got out and made some friends who helped me get a divorce from him." Tasha takes a big swig of her drink.

Tasha's stories leave the group speechless. Rita notices a barely palpable tension between herself and Tasha.

When the evening ends, Rita and Tasha walk out to the garden together. Tasha smokes and Rita sits down on a bench in warm air that smells of jasmine and cigarettes. Few words are spoken between them. A silence that comes from the dark connects them. All of a sudden Tasha starts to cry. Rita puts her arm around Tasha as her body shakes with her sobs. Neither woman understands the exchange, but they both allow the intimacy without question.

On the last day of the conference, several of the women, including Tasha and Rita, meet for dinner. They will all fly home the next morning. The group heads into the old part of San Diego where they find a Mexican restaurant and order margaritas with their dinners. The conversation moves around many subjects and rests upon the topic of past lives and memories from past lives.

Tasha reports working with a psychic in Florida. "I was living in Ireland," Tasha begins. "A successful businessman who smoked cigars. I was quite a womanizer. I really liked being a man." Tasha winks and a sly smile spreads across her face.

"I can understand that attitude," thinks Rita, "given Tasha's current life experiences, especially in Russia."

Others around the table express their experiences with past lives, but Rita keeps her knowledge to herself. She feels the life you are currently living is the one that is important, although she finds the idea of past lives interesting. It's just that they are irrelevant to Rita except when they impact the life one is currently experiencing.

The next day Rita flies home. While driving the final leg of her journey, Rita's mind is flooded with a memory. It is always incredible to Rita when she receives information like this. It is as if the veils are removed from her mind and she can see directly into life without any barriers. As she drives, an image comes to her. It is of Tasha as a man in Ireland and Rita as a dancer. Rita is married to a man Rita recognizes as Roberto in her current life. The husband works all the time and is never available. The dancer and businessman are married and love each other tremendously but his work draws him away from her. She is lonely and finds comfort in the arms of the playboy whom Rita has just met as Tasha.

As the dancer and the playboy, they have an affair and the man becomes very fond of her. He really likes her for more than just their sexual connection. He actually cares for her. The dancer's husband finds out about the affair and during a passionate encounter he breaks the dancer's neck.

Rita's consciousness watches the scene as it unfolds in front of her awareness. The husband can't believe he has just killed his wife, but she never moves again. She watches as he promises her dead body, "I will never love again." As the dancer, Rita's consciousness floats above the dead body and she hears and feels the words, "I will always love you. You cannot kill LOVE."

Rita arrives at home and can hardly believe what she sees as she glimpses reality. "How interesting," she thinks. "Roberto was flying to Ireland when I met him."

Rita has been unable to understand the connection she feels with Roberto and the pain that surrounds her experience with him. This peek into a different reality illuminates Rita's mind with a deeper understanding of life and all that transpires within each moment.

By now, the connection she experiences with Roberto in the physical is minimal. They connect only occasionally and Rita feels the separation. She also feels a deeper connection with the truth of the experience and the energy of Oneness. She continues to love the man Roberto, but starts to let go of the possibility of ever seeing him again. After all, he only makes excuses and Rita is not interested in excuses. She feels excuses are for people unwilling to assume responsibility or unconscious about their life experiences. This happens mostly through the deceptive nature of the ego that dominates most of humanity, keeping them separate from the truth that lies within the heart and surface experience.

Rita begins to tire of this experience with Roberto, for the lack of true expression begins to freeze the flow of her love. She no longer feels the heat of love between them and so patterns start to harden into a cold disconnection. Rita feels there is a possibility of freeing her soul through this experience with Roberto.

Rita knows she needs to keep her heart and mind open and aligned with a willingness to Love No Matter What. She continues to call Roberto and leave messages. He never returns the calls. This becomes the normal interaction between them. Rita stays connected to the flow of energy and consciousness because somewhere within she knows the flow of love will eventually free her heart, unifying the form with the formless.

The past-life awareness and its sensations remain acute in Rita's mind but eventually begin to fade into her body, opening a space that flows like a clean pure river into the Oneness of the ocean. The ice starts to melt and as it does, the outer disconnection melts into the Truth of Oneness. She recognizes that she does not need the outer world to acknowledge or recognize the state of Oneness. She needs only to hold the awareness of this and Be it no matter what occurs in the physical world. This is the only way her heart will become free from the pain of separation. An experience that starts with two is now becoming an experience of ONE.

# Oneness

There is no you
And there is no me
It was an illusion that was made within the mind
That we were ever separate
You were born from this illusion and when I
Experienced myself as separate
The pain was so great
I wanted to die more than I wanted to live

Within the moment I experienced the Truth
There was no you and there was no me

Most of one's experience is separation
It is not the Truth
But an illusion created by the mind
And lived by most

I will never experience you again
As separate, for the illusion has
Dissolved and the Truth is what is lived

There is no one to call
No one to see, no one to feel
No one to press their lips against
This too was an illusion born of separation.

I breathe in and am filled with you
I breathe out and I am connected with
ALL THAT IS

The consciousness of Oneness Rita experiences impacts all her relationships. Long ago, she recognized that relationships between herself and others, as well as between herself and material goods, need to be dynamic. To Rita, this meant not becoming attached to them but relating to them as part of her life and experience. Rita is aware that human beings identify themselves with the physical world, whether it be their bodies, their feelings, their roles (mother, father, doctor, lawyer, sister, brother), or material objects (their house, their car, their children, their spouse). This identification limits relationships to patterns and does not allow dynamic interaction. Relationships are not based on flow or interchange between awareness and what is being experienced. They become a need to "control and keep the same" in order to feel safe.

This identification with the physical world extends into relationships with others. Rita notes that people tend to seek out others who are similar to themselves in order to limit their own inner discomfort with differences. It is strange to Rita that most people she is in contact with have a very different awareness and experience of the physical world and themselves.

In the consciousness of Oneness, change happens easily because nothing is fixed or stationary. Oneness is dynamic and natural in its flow. It doesn't need to be forced or contrived. This of course illuminates the places within Rita that want something to happen or the parts of her that want to control the outcome of something. In particular, this Oneness surfaces within Rita's psyche when she thinks about seeing Roberto in physical form again. Her desire and willfulness to create a form within her relationship with Roberto is a constant source of conflict with the energy of Oneness. From what Rita can see, the collective psyche of humanity is also in constant conflict with the consciousness of Oneness.

Rita experiences this as personal, but also as something that exists in the world around her. She works through the barriers that manifest themselves within her, and more possibilities open in the world around her. She allows the image of Roberto to dissolve and welcomes the consciousness of Oneness and its awareness to flow more freely within her body, psyche and life. This energy connects all things without judgment, greed, domination, or the need to control. It allows a deep peace to settle into Rita's body and mind, opening her to new possibilities.

Rita's dynamic consciousness of Oneness is not threatening to Chris. He and Rita have been together for many years and Chris has learned to trust the integrity of the dynamic flow of Oneness that connects all life. Most people spend time and energy defending themselves against intimate contact. They derive safety from the images they place upon their partners. Rita recognizes that another person can never bring safety to her, nor does she expect such things. Feeling safe develops over time, through conscious and direct experience with life. Through our intimate connections with the natural world we feel the constant interconnections. Through these sensate experiences we know we are part of the dynamic flow, not separate from it.

Rita is in constant interaction with life—through the

food she prepares, when she touches her animals, or tends the plants surrounding her home. She senses the textures, colors, aromas and life force as she prepares dinner, recognizing the food's connection with all that is. This awareness brings the flavors, colors, textures, and beauty of the food to life. Chris sits down to dinner, breathing in the aromas of the food, taking in the beautiful way it has been prepared with gratitude and love. As Chris chews, his mouth waters and he absorbs the love within the food, recognizing the Oneness between the food, his wife Rita, and himself.

Rita insists on clear interactions with Chris. These interactions bring Chris closer to Rita and a direct experience of himself brings him closer to his true nature. Chris does not always find his relationship with Rita easy because she demands honesty. Honesty with oneself is not effortless. It requires a person to be willing to experience all levels of an interaction with presence. It requires a person be willing to experience emotions or sensate uncomfortable feelings. Honesty requires being with all of the experience without separating from it—just because something is not the way they want it to be. In Truth, people are just the way that they are. Our reactions to each other tend to separate us at different levels. Chris might experience an emotion like anger or fear that challenges his image of a loving partner. Rita is aware of this separation and sometimes brings Chris into its awareness with a question such as, What are you feeling? The reaction might vary, but eventually Chris connects with his "yes" to life and love and unifies his experience within himself. This is what eventually brings about a sense of deep trust with life and oneself. This flow of consciousness moving through Rita sparks growth in Chris and others who say "yes" to life's experience and find strength within the "yes" rather than the "no."

Rita continues to call Roberto but never makes contact. She continues to share her process with him on voice mail. Most of the time she feels like she is talking into a big, open space where there is no one at the other end to receive the message. This feeling moves into a reality of the impersonal experience. Rita goes through all the usual sensations of rejection and questioning herself, but decides to stay with the awareness of Oneness and not sever the connection made between them.

When she sits quiet in meditation, Rita finds a belief, an imprint upon her soul that says, "If a human being has a direct experience with Divine Love they will always choose it." But this is not what Rita experiences. She experiences Roberto turning his back upon the direct experience of Divine Love.

It is still difficult for Rita to be objective with Roberto because the interaction seems so intimate and personal. This is not where the energy has taken Rita, but it still feels personal through the sensual body, making it difficult to witness it from a place of complete objectivity. She has nothing to reflect this awareness against except empty space that she speaks into but only hears an echo back, "I love you." The effect is strange to Rita, but she is inwardly guided to continue to allow the experience.

Rita's life shifts its balance and she finds she does not have the need to work as much as she did. She connects more deeply with her garden, animals, and the earth. Rita's heart becomes larger as she continues to venture into the open space that contains both nothing and everything at the same time.

Rita is acutely aware of how separate most of humanity is from nature, the earth and its natural life rhythms and cycles. She observes this separation in her workplace as well as in most facets of the Western world dream being lived these days. This piques her ever-curious mind. How does the rest of the world connect with this energy of ONENESS? How does humanity connect to earth, which is crying out for help?

Rita and Chris enjoy the outdoors. They feel connected to the touch of the ground beneath their feet, the sounds of birds that awaken them in the morning, the new green growth that surrounds their home. They feel connected to the ever-changing sky. They feel part of the flow of life that surrounds them, moves through them, and caresses them—especially when they make love together.

It takes determination for Rita to stay aware of the consciousness of Oneness while interacting with others and within her workplace. She becomes aware that every part of her work environment has removed itself from what is natural. The human part of work and relationships with others is the only thing that still seems to have contact with living, moving matter. These surface interactions are guarded and not always honest, but they are required for the completion of their work. In fact, the complexities of systems created by man are still dependent on human interactions with each other in order to function.

Wherever Rita has been employed—private industry,

Non-Governmental Organization or government— communication is always the most important factor for efficient work and production. She also witnessed how rare it is to find honest and conscious communication. She also knows people respond to honest communication; even if they don't like what is said, there is always a response. Rita has gotten much better at communicating over the years. Many times she felt as though she might lose her job due to her efforts at honest communication, but she never was fired from any position she held. She feels Truth, even if it isn't what people want, awakens something real in them, which allows a connection.

Rita also recognizes that what is True for her is not always True for others, but it is the experience she is having and she finds it helps to connect to the moment as it occurs.

Most people are so guarded in their experience of life, so fearful of having life actually touch them, that they form a cocoon around themselves, manifesting insulation to avoid experiencing life within the moment. The mind constantly separates them from the experience of the sensate world.

Rita has traveled to so many places and found almost everywhere that people are disconnected from their immediate environment. She believes if people were actually awake within their lives they would feel the energy of Oneness and stop making bad choices that harm life energies.

Rita recalls being in New York City, sitting in a park, trying to center herself. She picks a tree to connect with, feeling into the bark, into the roots down in the ground and into the branches reaching up toward the sun and blue sky. As she connects with really seeing the tree—the texture of its bark, the smell of its leaves—she starts to find the center of herself. She notices how easy it was to become disconnected with her center when in the city. The constant noise, smells, sounds, and sights split her attention. She watches the dogs entering the park, tail between their legs, shaking, inundated with all the external input that overwhelms their sensitive bodies. They do not have the armor that people do to defend themselves against the unnatural barrage of input from the environment.

Rita observes how the animals are so clearly connected with their environment through all their senses. It is as if humans have barricaded themselves away from the city noise through their iPods, cell phones, computers, text messaging and twittering. All these technological advancements, meant to help people connect with one another, also seem to be increasing isolation and disconnection from the natural world. As humans draw closer in one aspect, they separate in another, illuminating the dualistic consciousness that continues to be present on the planet.

For the past forty years of Rita's life she has been feeling the earth moan with pain. She has witnessed the advances in technology from the first television and first walk on the moon, to Bluetooths and computers everywhere in the world. Does being plugged into the Internet equate to being connected into the energy of ONENESS?

Rita feels the question her mind poses, 'Does it equate to being connected to ONENESS?' They mirror each other, but something very real is missing from the connectedness of the Internet and the connectedness she feels with the earth and nature.

ONENESS for Rita is both an inner- and outer-connected

experience. She feels at one with the outer experience of life and connects with the soul of the earth and depth of her own heart and soul. Her experience with Roberto helped to bridge the inner and outer worlds for Rita. She no longer feels separate from any of life even though she lives in a world that appears utterly separate and disconnected from the reality she is living

Roberto and Rita have no outer connection anymore, but she does not feel a disconnect. She feels the connection with the energy of Oneness in all things—the air that moves across her skin, the heat of the sun in her bones, the smell of the sea, the reflection of light off new leaves in her garden. Rita listens to the inner silence and hears birds singing within her very being. This is what makes Rita feel alive—being a part of everything that is witnessed and experienced.

Rita looks within her mind and heart for the individual Roberto was before he disappeared from her outer experience and no longer takes up any space within her. How can that be, she contemplates. Something that was so important, so real—how can that completely vanish?

But it has; Roberto is nowhere to be found. He is only an illusion to be experienced and lost in order to bring Rita into the state of being that she comes to know as ONENESS.

She tries for months to talk with Roberto to no avail. His image of being separate from her drops away from the imprint of separation that has been upon her soul from the beginning. No longer does her mind wander into the state of separation, away from the moment being experienced. If she remains absolutely present in the moment with all her senses there is no separation, no pain. Only the here and now, which is unfolding, dynamic, and current with what IS. Being immersed within the experience of one's life allows Rita to be completely alive, completely connected, and part of the dynamic flow and current that is being created as she experiences it.

This allows everything Rita experiences to be alive with the ability to change—completely dynamic, completely alchemical. She experiences the profound freedom of this state of Oneness that threatens most everything that is manmade and separate from this dynamism of life's currents.

Rita not only becomes part of this flow of Oneness; she is aware of its impact on the world around her. Rita has deep awareness that the very DNA structure of her physical body is now being affected by this flow of ONENESS, allowing something she doesn't understand and cannot predict or control to happen. A mystery is currently unfolding and she is participating in its creation. This is not something happening only with Rita, but all around the world in all areas of the world. The natural world is changing and becoming increasingly unpredictable. Manmade systems that have been functioning are slowly coming to a standstill, a silent halt, a quiet death.

Rita has no fear of change, for she feels connected with change, not separate from it. The connection with life itself gives Rita a comfort and Peace that is deep and far-reaching. All around her, people voice their fears. Fear of changes entering into the world, economic security becoming a myth, job security becoming a myth—all types of change seem to threaten people's sense of safety. Fear has separated human beings from their experience with life, making them part of a frozen reality conjured up within their minds rather than part of the dynamic breath of life. As the consciousness of Oneness pushes itself into the world, it seems to shake the ground that humans have built their lives on.

# Endings

Completion of a cycle,
There may be nothing left that is recognizable

But in that nothing there is everything
All of its parts have been connected
Threaded together with the finest gold

While on the journey it may have felt endless
Insurmountable, with no end in sight
Finally the circle closes complete unto itself
Containing everything and nothing

It is an exhale
As in death our last breath is always
An inhale back to the source
The inspiration of all that is

As this cycle completes itself we await for
The inspiration to begin something new.

As time unfolds and the natural rhythm of life continues, what has been experienced with Roberto becomes woven into the background of Rita's life. It is no longer a prominent point that everything else revolves around. It blends into the understanding that all things are One regardless of how they may appear to the person having the experience. When all personal attachments fall away there is ONE, nothing dividing the experience with the one having the experience. Rita becomes the witness of a perfectly choreographed dance between the dancer and the dance of life. There may be a new tempo to the music, a new step to learn, a new partner to embrace, but it is all ONE— One endless dance in the spirals that flow through life. Rita finally is part of this sense of ONENESS and begins to be part of the dance, observing and being part of its beauty.

Chris's mother, Emma, who lives in Southern California, becomes ill quite suddenly. Emma is in her seventies and lives in the house where Chris and his brother and sister, John and Sandy, grew up. Emma has been independent and happy in her routine. She is a widow who enjoyed a second relationship with a man named Rick after her husband Harvey died. Rick died a number of years ago and Emma has been alone since then. Emma has bleached blonde hair and a twinkling set of blue eyes. It is easy to see she was an attractive woman in her younger days. Emma took up smoking in her twenties and enjoyed it, but when her first grandson was born, her family was adamant that she stop smoking if she wished to spend time with him. Emma met Ryan and fell in love with the boy. She quit smoking soon after she held her grandson for the first time. Emma has been smoke free for the past two years.

Emma has been plagued with back and neck pain for as long as Rita can remember. Emma's complaints are a normal part of their interactions. In January, Emma's back pain became intolerable and she decided to try some form of injection therapy rather than rely on her usual pain pills. The stress of being in unrelenting pain, her lifetime habit of smoking, and the injection therapy triggered a lung condition called pulmonary fibrosis. Emma has experienced a rapid decline in her ability to breathe. She requires oxygen therapy and large doses of prednisone to slow down the rapidly progressing pulmonary fibrosis.

Rita and Chris visit Emma in March. It is obvious to Rita that Emma does not have much time left. They had seen Emma on their way to a vacation destination, and again on their return two weeks later. There is noticeable worsening in Emma's condition in just these two weeks. When Rita and Chris return to their home, they sit on the deck overlooking the forest and beyond—out over the ocean and on to the horizon. The sun is setting and the sky is shades of lavender and amber. They absorb the beauty of the moment. They remain silent for a while then Rita says, "I want to take care of your mother as she dies."

Chris looks at Rita with his soft, open eyes. "Really?" he says.

"I can easily make time in my work schedule to be with her. I think she will be more comfortable with me than you or your brother John. Your sister, Sandy, hasn't spoken to your mom in fifteen years." Rita feels her heart directing her to speak and her head surrenders to the guidance of her heart without question.

They call Emma. "I want to come down to Southern California and take care of you as you die," Rita tells Emma.

"Really?" says Emma.

Rita simply says, "Yes."

Emma relaxes with gratitude and says, "Thank you."

Rita allows herself to listen deep inside in order to respond to the moment as it unfolds.

It is May and Mother's Day weekend. Chris and his siblings fly down to visit Emma. It is the first time Chris's sister, Sandy, has seen Emma in fifteen years. They have not been on speaking terms all that time. Emma is grateful to see her daughter and they make a meaningful connection during the visit. Chris also enjoys having his siblings and mother together; it brings back warm memories of childhood.

"My sister could always make me laugh. My sides are sore from laughing so much," Chris says to Rita when he calls home.

Rita asks a few questions. Is your mom eating? What is her oxygen set at? How much activity is she able to handle?

"She only picks at her food. Her oxygen is set on six liters. She can walk between her bedroom and living room before needing to rest. We needed to use a wheel chair when we went out to lunch."

Rita takes in this information and again listens deep inside herself. With a sense of deep clarity, Rita makes plane reservations to take her down to California go stay with Emma. Physical death is predictable in that it happens to all of life, but how and when is not predictable. It is part of the mystery of life and many factors determine its ending. Rita prepares to spend a couple of weeks there, then plans to hire someone to stay with Emma. Rita will return home to work and then fly back to Emma's home as she's needed.

Rita plans this as she listens to the depth of wisdom rising out of her heart. She follows her heart explicitly. Emma's friend Kat picks Rita up from the airport. Kat is a tremendous help to Emma during this time. Kat is Emma's closest friend and Rita and Kat liked each other from the start.

Emma's face is swollen from the prednisone and the oxygen tubing is pressing into her round cheeks. She is glad to see Rita; her shoulders drop visibly in relaxation. Emma uses all her accessory muscles to breathe, adding new lines of stress to her face and mouth as she purses her lips.

Rita slows down her pace in order to synchronize with Emma's pace. She sits with Emma and asks if there are people she wants to see. Emma has always been quite social and enjoys her friendships.

"I would like to have the Friday Girls over one more time," Emma gasps. "We do wine and appetizers at 5:30 p.m. every Friday evening. We've been doing it for years. Kat comes and she can help you get in touch with the other women. I think I need to lie down."

Emma puts her legs up on the coach and tries to get comfortable. Rita prepares for Friday evening. She shops and cooks to provide a festive atmosphere for these friends. Emma has a hard time walking from her bedroom to the living room now. Her shortness of breath gets worse each day. The lines of fatigue around her eyes are growing deeper and Rita knows Emma will not stay in her body much longer. Friday comes and the "girls" enjoy their time with Emma. Most conversations stay superficial, but in their hearts they know their friend is dying.

Emma spends more time in bed. Rita asks, "Do you have any letters to write?"

Rita writes as Emma dictates her thoughts and feelings. Each day her strength diminishes. Recognizing that leaving one's life is difficult, Rita asks, "Do you feel complete with everything?"

Emma speaks slowly and gasps for breath between the words. "I feel complete with my relationships with my children and friends, but I love this house and this neighborhood. I love the view from the living room window."

Rita listens and is guided to the next step.

Rita goes through every closet and cupboard in Emma's house. She asks Emma where she wants each item to go after she dies. When the last item is accounted for, Emma becomes quiet.

Rita calls Chris and his brother John to let them know the time is near. Chris's brother wants to see his mom again and be with her when she passes. He flies down and spends time at Emma's bedside. She is in her bed now most of the time and has a view of the photos displayed on her dresser.

Rita will be leaving on Friday and so she hires a person to stay with Emma. It is Wednesday morning and Rita sits on the bed next to Emma. Emma is quiet, her eyes closed.

"What are you doing?" Rita asks.

"I'm meditating," Emma replies.

Rita is curious. "What about?"

"I am mad at God for Harvey dying and I am mad about Rick dying and about my relationship with my daughter, Sandy."

Rita is quiet for a long moment. "Did you ever think life and all the things we experience are to help us learn about love?"

"No."

"If Harvey hadn't died, would you have met Rick?"

"No."

"Did you learn how to love Rick more than you ever loved Harvey?"

"Yes."

"Did you ever stop loving Sandy even though she wouldn't allow a relationship with you?"

"No," replies Emma.

A profound silence comes over the room and Rita sees what looks like a drop of sunlight into a dark pool within her mind. Rita looks at Emma and says, "Do you feel that?"

"What?"

"That Peace."

"Yes, I think I do," says Emma.

Rita feels something like a fine mist penetrating a parched desert and is struck by the beauty of what has just occurred. Rita goes out for a run every day and takes the opportunity to run now. When she returns, John is sitting with Emma. It is clear that Emma is starting to move out of her physical body.

The hospice nurse will be arriving later in the day to provide phone numbers and medications. Rita and John read poetry, play Botticelli's music on the CD player and sit in silence listening to Emma's breath become more labored. Rita is sitting on the bed next to Emma and John is in a chair as Emma draws in her last breath.

The circle of Emma's life completes itself on Thursday night. Rita prepares to fly home as scheduled on Friday morning at 8 a.m. John drives Rita to the airport. They recognize the beauty of Emma's final days and hug each other.

Rita nestles back into the seat of the plane and rests within her heart holding the experience as part of Oneness. Feeling blessed, she falls asleep.

Back at home, Rita rests in Chris's arms and they allow the experience to unfold between them. Chris is connected to the experience through Rita's heart and allows his loss and gratitude to be felt as One flowing feeling. They recount the blessing for Emma that she did not have to linger in death for very long, that she was able to leave her body, returning it to the earth from which it came. Rita and Chris fall asleep together in a peaceful silence after the tears have been shed and the loss has been felt.

Having worked in healthcare for years, Rita often witnesses how difficult it is for people to have a "good death." She recognizes that good deaths take place less often as human life becomes more technical and more removed from the natural rhythms of life. Death is included in the natural rhythms of life. Rita understands that the Western world is so attached to its physicality and materialism that it no longer remembers death is part of the natural rhythm of life and so it becomes difficult for many undergoing the transition. The basic TRUTHS known and lived by indigenous people are no longer part of the collective understanding of life.

Rita recalls the story of the Eskimo woman who reviews her life and sees that she is taking more than she is able to give. She walks out onto the ice field and is eaten by a polar bear. The polar bear is killed in a hunt, which feeds her family, nourishing their bellies. The bear's pelt keeps them warm against the icy wind. She is now ONE with them. This cycle of life and death returning consciously and willingly back into the earth has nurtured the cycle of life upon this planet until recently.

More common now is that the balance of life and death is interrupted by the human need to control and dominate these forces. Rita looks out at the ocean, feeling the sun upon her face. She smells the breeze, knowing she is one with all of life.

# Inspiration

It stands on its own
Strong and tall, quiet and solitude
When everything else falls away
It comes from within

A known source within the unknown
A spark of light
In the midst of darkness
Lighting the way through fear and chaos

Illuminating the darkness
Independent of the outer world
It brings something new into creation
When everything else has been lost and

No longer brings meaning to the soul of the world
It is carried like a seed of light within the heart
Waiting to be born, waiting to give life

Finally, when the moment comes
It is exhaled into manifestation
Giving birth to a whole new world.

Rita continues to connect with the feelings awakened within her by Roberto. The feelings are a pure love, white, untainted by the physical world. She allows the feelings to burn away all illusion, all impurities within her mind and body. The pain of not making physical contact diminishes like a shadow that dissolves within the light of love burning within Rita's heart and soul.

Rita finds herself seeing everything within the world as different. No longer are things divided by right and wrong, good and bad. They form around the understanding of "this is how it is," a deep surrender into the moment currently being experienced. No longer does she have the need to try to change something or have it look different or be different from what it is. This profound acceptance filters into the cells of her body, into her mind, and down into how she lives her life. Struggles between herself and her outer experiences diminish, bringing a peacefulness that penetrates Rita's life.

Rita never gives much thought to how others perceive her, for she has always seen and felt herself as different and never tried to become something she wasn't. She is used to living her life based on her internal beat and notices that her rhythm is different from the rest of the world's, not through separation, but through unity of these differences. She has done this for so long that it has become a natural state within Rita's experience of herself. She never expects the rest of the world to join in, but often looks for others who move to a different rhythm. Rita often makes friends with people who are a bit different from the average person. She likes people who play notes differently from the background music most people play. Even when she connects with others who play the chorus of the collective, she looks for something unusual within them. It is always their uniqueness that brings inspiration to Rita. She is not inspired by those who hum the tune of the collective without recognition of their own unique note, or voice, or ability.

Rita is at work and needs to screen a client through the clinic's interview process. The client is in his mid-forties and presents to the clinic with acute physical problems. He is homeless and has been hitchhiking down the West Coast. He carries a backpack and has a dog companion for the journey. The clinic staff is used to seeing homeless people. These people are generally categorized as alcoholic, drug addicted, or crazy. When the caseload is divided among the staff, Rita usually picks up these cases.

Because of her experience with the criminally insane, Rita feels more comfortable facing this aspect of humanity than most people would. Rita walks into the room, spraying antiseptic on her hands before greeting Bruce because she does not know what to expect. She is on the lookout for common characteristics of addictive behavior and psychotic features. But because Rita does not fear these aspects of humanity, she is able to enter the room relaxed and present. This demeanor often helps homeless clients—especially those with psychotic features—relax a bit themselves.

Rita starts with the usual questions. When she asks if he is homeless, Bruce says, "I don't like to call myself homeless. I prefer the word 'transient.' Most homeless people are alcoholic, drug-addicted and don't work. I'm transient only because I am unsure where I want to live."

Rita is intrigued by the way Bruce articulates this statement, and decides she wants to know his story. Her job requires only that she stick with basic interview questions, not detour into the personal story of someone's life. But as a human being, she is interested in his story. Bruce seems to be playing a different note and she wants to hear his sound within her heart.

Rita sees Bruce's backpack propped up against the wall. It is old and well-used, but tidy.

"How long have you been transient?" Rita asks.

"Since my wife's death, my dog and I have been traveling west from Kentucky."

"Where is your dog?"

"She is at the animal shelter. They've agreed to keep her until I come and get her."

"What did you do before your wife died?"

"I was a meteorologist in the Bay Area when my wife became ill."

"Where did you go to school?"

"Rutgers. I have two degrees; the second is in art history."

Bruce is missing a front tooth and has tattoos on both arms. His shoulder-length hair is clean. He has long sideburns and wears eyeglasses held together with tape.

"My wife got cancer and she went through all the treatments available. When she became severely ill, I began taking a lot of time off from work. My boss said I couldn't have any more time off. I quit my job and moved my wife back to Kentucky, where my wife's family lives. When she died I felt lost, unsure of what I was going to do next."

Rita asked if he ever felt depressed or suicidal.

"Sure," he said. "I feel depressed all the time and once I felt suicidal. I had a dream where my dog was sitting in front of me and she kept getting smaller and further away. When I realized my dog would have no one to take care of her if I was gone, I realized I could not leave her and the suicidal feelings stopped. I took off walking across the country and hitchhiking, and occasionally working to get money. After my wife died, an insurance company called and wanted to know when I was going to pay off the thirty thousand dollars I owed them. I told them my wife just died. The man said, 'I guess we'll have to wait until you die and we can get your organs donated.' That was the last straw. I became so disillusioned with humanity at that point that I had no desire to return to the mainstream of life. I just couldn't. It's not what I believe in."

"It sounds like you are listening to something deep inside yourself and it helps direct you in life," Rita said quietly.

"I was walking along in Tennessee and it was pouring rain," Bruce says. "I wasn't looking for a ride but this woman in an old, beat-up car pulls alongside me and asks if I want a ride. I really preferred to walk, but there is a little girl in the back seat crying and something tells me to get into the car, so I got in. I turned around and asked the little girl why she is crying. These people are really poor; the woman doesn't even have a pair of shoes. She tells me her little girl has a toothache. They had just come from a church down the way to see if they could get some money for the dentist, but the church turned them away. I said, 'I bet we can find a dentist to pull the tooth for what I have in my pocket.' We stopped at a payphone booth and I make some calls. I find a dentist that will pull the tooth for seventy dollars. After that, the mother insists I come home with them and she would fix me something to eat. I return home with her. As she is preparing dinner, she tells me to help myself to something to drink in the refrigerator. The only thing in the refrigerator is a milk container filled with an orange drink. I tell the lady, 'I don't think you'll be able to fix me anything I want, let's go to the grocery store.' I had another hundred dollars in my pocket and used that money to buy groceries for this woman and her daughter. We eat a meal together and I leave the next day. You know, ever since that day I've felt I've had something watching out for me."

"I think what you are looking for has always been with you," Rita says.

Bruce has a couple more stories he needs to share with Rita, which she listens to and then ends the interview. The interview inspires Rita. She didn't stop when viewing the outer appearance of Bruce, or at what her colleagues surmised about the man. She is open to the experience of Bruce and finds a beautiful caring heart that cannot understand the outside world and how it is manifesting itself around him. He sees and experiences himself and expresses that self in a way that does not merge or unify with the outer world. Rita does not feel the need to change Bruce's experience. He is finding his way through the world in his own unique way. Rita simply feels and sees him with her heart. She does bring him a bag of dog food, some organic apples and almonds, and a small clear rose quartz crystal to assist him on the next part of his journey.

Rita knows Bruce is listening to something deep within his heart and she feels it is important to recognize and witness this "something" for him. She knows that others will not see the same thing that she does, but it does not matter. The Truth of the situation within the moment is as he tells the story and, in what Rita feels in her heart, nothing more and nothing less. What is important to Rita is to see and understand life from a clear and discerning heart, not from concepts that lie within the mind.

# The Heart That Loves

Each time I reach out in love
It fills the air around me
With a fragrance soft and sweet

It never reaches you
So I reach out again

The love in the heart
Starts to fill the world

I reach out again
And the world starts to change

It is this constant pull of the heart
Filled with love that changes the world

That love may never touch your lips again
The heart free to love continues to reach into the world

The heart no longer looks to be met by you
For it has found its beloved
In LOVE itself.

Rita loves to work outside and she plants the land surrounding her home with native shrubs and flowers to enrich the natural landscape of trees and ferns. Already out there are huckleberry, twinberry, St John's Wart, native azaleas, myrtle wood, and wild rhododendron. The birds fly and sing on the land surrounding her.

Several varieties of lavender are planted on the south side of her home. When the lavender blooms, she hears the hum of honeybees working the purple blossoms. But this year, Rita can count the bees on one hand. Rita's heart is heavy with the knowledge that so much of life is dying. The natural world that brings comfort to her heart and soul is dropping away at such a rapid pace that her heart aches and her eyes flow with tears whenever she feels life move through her body without its rich breath.

This awareness never leaves Rita's consciousness because she feels connected to life through nature. It is where Rita feels the heart beat of the world. She feels it in every living plant, every animal and mineral, and she feels it as part of her own being. She has many dreams about animals and the planet.

Rita works to help people in order to earn a living, but her nourishment comes from the natural world. People have become so far removed from nature that they no longer move with its rhythm. Rita observes that the world is becoming more and more out of balance in every aspect. She is aware of the ecological movements and that many communities are moving toward healthier lifestyles, but the masses of humanity seem to turn their backs on the very thing they are made of—the earth itself.

Most indigenous cultures have recognized animals as their relatives. They know animals come from the earth, giving them knowledge and understanding about life through their connection with the earth. They are aware that the way they treat the earth will have a direct effect on them. Somehow, for modern culture, this basic connection between the earth and humanity got lost. The need to dominate and control nature became much more important than the wisdom that came from their ancestors or from simply observing and being within the context of their surroundings.

Rita always tries to listen to the environment, so she and Chris spend their time hiking, backpacking, or in the ocean and waterways harmonizing with nature's natural rhythm. This helps them to stay connected to nature's rhythm within their own bodies. Rita tries hard to maintain a sense of balance within her life as the world around her becomes more unbalanced. She is aware that when the environment is running smoothly and effortlessly in its natural rhythmic cycles, the body is supported by these rhythmic pulsations of life. They are constant, but as the web that connects all of life breaks apart it is harder to feel the supportive pulsation that nurtures the essence of Being.

Rita and Chris are conversing about life as they watch the sun setting over the Pacific Ocean. They breathe in the beauty of colors and the fragrance of the forest and let the last rays of sun warm their skin before retreating inside their home. Rita remembers a dream from her childhood. She hadn't thought of the dream for years, but the conversation with Chris brought the dream to the surface of her mind.

Rita and Chris sit down together on the couch. Rita curls up next to Chris. "During my childhood I had a repeating vision that came through a dream. I had the dream until I was eleven years old."

Chris remains quiet and listens as Rita continues.

"This dream abruptly stopped coming to me when my family moved from New York to California and I started my period. Actually, the dream only came to me while we lived in that one house in New York. The land the house stood on was once home to Native Americans, with whom I have always felt akin."

Rita lapses into silence. She wonders if the vision came from the land itself or from within her soul, like a point of memory guiding her life. Both may be true; the land helps the memory come to life through the dream, pointing and guiding the person like a compass to its destination.

"We are now at that time within the vision that the dream is pointing to," Rita says.

Chris rubs Rita's feet as she tells him the content of the dream. "The world becomes so polluted that there is no clean water to drink; the air tastes like exhaust fumes. The trees and vegetation have been disregarded for their beauty and majesty. They are seen only for their economic value, not for the integral part they play within the balance of life. No longer are the trees able to bring sufficient oxygen or rain in many parts of the world. What will the timber be sold for? What will the crops bring in at harvest time? Their value as part of the living, breathing web of life is overshadowed by their monetary value. The vision progresses within the dream and there is diminishing wild land; cities of concrete and skyscrapers fill the vision. The horizon is filled with cityscapes and smog with very little natural life. In the dream, I watch as man destroys the planet through his ignorance. Then another planet that can support human life is discovered and most of humanity leaves the Earth to inhabit the other place. A few humans remain behind, mostly indigenous people that feel they are a part of the Earth. The rest of those who stay are somehow called to remain upon this planet."

Rita takes a sip of water before she continues to share the dream with Chris. "Those that stay on the Earth form a governmental system that holds all of life as one being and makes choices based on the whole. The Earth responds in a magical way. Its natural beauty returns so quickly that the man-made cities crumble and trees spring up through the concrete. I watch, delighted as nature comes back to life and humans live within its harmony. A deep Peace settles within the human heart as the people learn how to relate to life and to each other from a state of ONENESS rather than individuation and personal will. In the dream, people begin to remember how to listen to the rhythms of life, nature and the earth again. They learn to make choices based on these rhythms. Harmony and magic return to the Earth and all the creatures that have remained on the planet. The humans that left for the other planet continue in their unconscious and selfish ways with no growth or change in behavior. They become more technologically advanced, but more removed from their human hearts and essential nature. It takes very little time before the water and air of the new planet become uninhabitable."

Another silence.

Chris takes in a deep breath in and touches Rita's arm as he feels what the dream means to him.

"The dream always ends at the same place," says Rita. "It ends with the technologically-advanced humans wanting to return to Earth. The guardians of the Earth are confronted with either allowing them to return and destroying the earth again, or fighting them off and in the process, destroying the harmony and state of Oneness that has been created in the heart of the Earth itself. My dream ends with this dilemma every time I dreamt this vision."

Chris and Rita are quiet as their hearts join and hold the dream together. Rita contemplates her vision in its vivid memory and knows in her heart that the Earth and humanity are experiencing this dilemma at that very moment.

"I know that the answer to the dilemma of the Earth and all its technological advancements is within the hearts of humans that inhabit the earth at this very time," Rita says. "The problem is, the majority of humanity does not live within their hearts; they live within the separation created by the human ego. They are driven by fear and ignorance, unable to touch the deep wisdom that unifies humanity with the earth."

"That's true," says Chris. "You can see this every day by the choices people make."

Rita never understands why she feels Oneness with Roberto, but as she reflects on her dream she feels the dream and her experience with Roberto are related. The consciousness of Oneness as it flows from one human heart to another is truly one of the most beautiful experiences Rita has ever felt. It is also one of the most painful experiences Rita has ever felt. The egos of both Rita and Roberto make the experience of Oneness painful. Through the mantra, "Love No Matter What," Rita learns how to hold the beauty of Divine Love and the pain of separation within her heart, not separating one from the other.

Both Rita and Roberto have a direct experience of Oneness. Oneness can only be experienced within the moment it is occurring. The nature within man's ego is to crystallize experiences into form. The crystallization process of the ego stops one from experiencing Oneness because our nature is to hold on, creating an illusion. Rita often sees this function of the ego when she works with people. The structure of our physical bodies holds many experiences, both pleasurable and painful. This process is largely unconscious and the structures of our bodies are reinforced by repeating the positive and negative experiences within our life. Humanity does not know or does not understand that for change to occur this structuring capacity of the ego needs to transform.

Again, people do not recognize this. They are controlled and made captive by their own ego that crystallizes them into form. This separates them from the real Truth of their Being, their Divine Essence. This constant reinforcement that structures mankind's ego has become so successful that man has come to know himself as separate from the earth and all of nature. It is an illusion that Rita experiences as painful. She feels the Truth within her heart that all of life is one breathing Spiritual Being. The illusion of this separate state is painful to live and experience. Humans have become so captivated by the illusion of themselves that they don't realize they are destroying themselves as the Earth and all of nature dies.

Rita does not share these thoughts with Chris; she simply holds the awareness within her heart, allowing the ocean of LOVE to caress her vision. Rita knows she is a witness to the Divine process occurring now as well as being part of it through life's experiences. Her body relaxes in Chris's arms. Their breath becomes synchronized, flowing through their bodies, out into the world, and then back into the source of life within their hearts. They witness this flow of breath, nourishing and connecting them with all of life.

# The Gift

A moment that transcends time and space
Where the inner and the outer are ONE

A shared moment with all of life
No separation, only a pulsing
Flowing timeless bridge
Connecting the Two worlds

That of creation and that of manifestation

Words can only bring you into the moment
Then there is a pulse between emptiness
And all of life

Rhythmically glowing
Feeding a network unifying the creative forces
With the manifest world AS ONE BEING

The masculine and feminine forces of
Giving and receiving in balanced harmony
Creates this pulse that feeds and connects
All of Life.

Rita tries to make sense of all her experiences, knowing that within the tapestry they create is an answer to the dilemma of the two worlds. At this moment, the clarity of the answer evades her awareness. One of Rita's favorite sayings by the Persian mystic, Rumi, is "Find the answer to the question in the question itself." Rita tries to formulate the question: What is needed to unify the world of technology with the natural world of creation? There may be a better question, but for now that is the question she ponders.

Rita also realizes that answers don't come immediately; they come when they are ready to be received and able to be understood. One of the difficulties Rita feels is humanity's lack of unified direction. As long as the individual is seen as most important, humanity will be blocked from seeing itself as One being. It will also continue the dream that humanity is living right now. But Rita also hears a note of hope, like a penetrating resonance that vibrates through each cell of her body. No matter how difficult a situation is or how overwhelming a task might be, that vibration penetrates the conscious mind and fills more space than visible matter. Rita doesn't always hear that note of hope, but she knows it is always there if she attunes to it.

Truly listening to something beyond the chatter of the superficial mind takes deep concentration, years of devoted meditation, and truly being present with one's current life situation. Rita is aware of this movement to quiet oneself. She sees its evidence on calendars and sayings posted at the end of e-mails. At the same time, the world of technology is changing so rapidly that it is causing changes in the natural world faster than its rhythms can accommodate.

The world is distorted, out of balance, wobbling rather than spinning harmoniously. Rita wonders if the increase in speed is what is needed to change the self-described direction to being One with all of life. A second question comes from the original, leading the way forward even when the destination is unknown. Change is entering one's life these days on many, many levels. The changes may not be what individuals want, but they are coming.

The information age, led by computers, puts the world into the hands of anyone with access to the Internet, a highway built in cyberspace that connects and builds relationships within the world community.

Rita again returns to her question, How can we connect the two worlds—the first world of matter and technology, the second world of the Creative Spirit that lives within all life and connects the Divine Web?

Several years ago, Rita went to New Mexico to attend a talk and meditation on Oneness given by Llewellyn Vaughan-Lee, a Sufi mystic and prolific author. Lee arranges gatherings that bring together people interested in exploring the Divine that arises from the hearts of those attending the meetings.

Rita loves the Southwest and knows that joining others around the topic of Oneness is important. Rita books a flight and arranges for a room in a hotel within walking distance of the gathering in the old, downtown part of Santa Fe. Rita has been to Santa Fe several times and she never tires of the people, culture, and land that influence her visits. Slightly more than two hundred people from all over the world attend that particular gathering.

Rita wakes up early, just as the sun is rising. It is fall, and the temperature is cold enough to see your breath at dawn. Rita dons gloves and a hat and starts out on a morning jog up into Santa Fe's Old Town section. No tourists are on the sidewalks. The streets are empty of cars. Rita's muscles warm up as blood pumps through her heart with increased speed. The birds are just waking up and the sun is rising, giving a golden-rose wash across the eastern sky.

Rita pays attention to the street signs so she can retrace her steps back to the hotel. She looks at her watch; she has been running for thirty minutes. She decides to turn around, heading back through the plaza. Rita passes the Mission and crosses the street. A woman is opening the door of a café as Rita rounds the corner. They greet, "Good morning," as a puff of warm air flows from the door of the café. Rita finds that people are less guarded when she makes contact with them before the day's tourists inundate their lives.

Rita reaches her hotel, stretches, showers, and makes a cup of coffee. She looks at the clock and sees she has time to eat breakfast before the meeting begins. Since she doesn't know where she is going, she gives herself a bit of extra time to get there. She gets directions from the hotel receptionist and sets out on foot for the meeting hall.

She concentrates on her breath and each step she is taking, bringing her body, mind, Spirit, and breath into the moment. Rita allows her breathing to deepen. She concentrates on her chest and its tender center. After several blocks of concentration, Rita arrives at the meeting hall. People are milling around outside in the sunshine and warming air. No longer are gloves and hat necessary. Rita doesn't know anyone there, so she enters the building and smiles as she pays the fee and picks up an agenda.

Rita wanders among tables of books and CDs and makes mental notes of the titles that interest her. Already many people area seated in the front rows. Rita finds a seat in the center of the second to last row. Her attention is focused on her heart as she sits down. She is aware of her surroundings and the people in the room but keeps her mind focused on her heart when Llewellyn Vaughn-Lee begins his talk.

Lee sits cross-legged in a chair on a stage a few steps higher than audience level. He wears a cream-colored sweater and pants. He has a full head of salt and pepper hair, a cropped beard, and wears small spectacles. He addresses the audience with a humble voice that Rita's heart attunes to readily. Rita has read several of Llewellyn's books and is acquainted with his mystical teachings. He addresses the intention of the talks and the consciousness of Oneness and answers several questions from the audience. This all sets an atmosphere to meditate together in silence. Numerous vibratory frequencies make up the meditation harmonizing within the consciousness of Oneness.

Rita enters a world of light. She has meditated for years and has experienced many levels of consciousness during meditation and lucid dreaming. The experience within this particular meditation is quite clear. Rita sees herself sitting in meditation when a woman in flowing lavender approaches. Rita recognizes the woman as her "higher self." The woman gives Rita two objects: a chartreuse purse and a white box decorated with silver and gold ribbons. The woman beckons Rita to follow her. Rita stands and walks behind the flowing lavender robes. She is led up a glass staircase to a large glass door. Rita opens the door and sees light beings constructing structures with crystalline blocks of light. She walks past them, feeling her heart beckoning her forward. She hears, "Trust your heart; it will take you where you need to go." As Rita walks, she finds herself moving along a spiraling pathway. Half the time Rita is in light and half the time she's in complete darkness. All along the path she hears and feels the words, "Follow your heart, it will lead you through the darkness." She continues to follow her heart and suddenly finds herself above Earth, in outer space. She is sitting cross-legged, meditation style. Rita looks into the night sky that is filled with stars and she waits. Rita then turns into a spider and falls into the center of the Earth. She spins an intricate web of light, reaching from the center of the Earth to its exterior. She returns to the center of the Earth, sits in the web as a woman, and notices that the silver and gold ribbons are gone from the box. They are woven into the web. Rita opens the chartreuse purse and finds it filled with diamonds sparkling with light. Rita scatters the diamonds throughout the web of light. She opens the white box and inside is a map that shows the way to her destination. It is a map home to Oneness, the Divine within her manifest form. Then Rita turns into a light and she merges with another light. They pulse together, which feeds the entire web outward and through small openings that bring light into the outer world.

As the meditation is ending, Rita finds herself back

outside on the surface of the planet. Her mind tells her she is in South America. She sees what look like electric cords getting unplugged, causing flashes of light and then darkness. The bell tones and the meditation ends.

Rita opens her eyes to a room full of people who also have just re-entered after meditation. The vision Rita has is shared with the group and settles into Rita as she tries to make sense of all that transpired in her vision. For the next several nights, Rita has interesting dreams that seem to have been spun off from the vision. She remembers her childhood dream and intuitively knows that somehow they are connected. Dreams and visions speak a very different language from that which the mind uses every day. Learning how they interact and make sense manifests something new as part of its creative process.

Rita returns home to Chris and they sit together enjoying dinner. Rita shares details of her trip to Santa Fe. Chris tells Rita of his experiences while she was gone. They reconnect with new excitement for one another, bringing together their separate experiences into one moment.

# Longing

An invisible pull between
What is loved and the One who Loves

A gravitational draw
Uniting two things together as ONE

Through a deep cry of the heart and soul
Being answered by an invisible light
That is felt through each and every living cell

The two come together
The light of their union
Illuminates the Truth that
All things are One and
Have always been One.

One day while Rita is in meditation she has the urge to call Roberto. He answers the phone. Rita hears, "I love you. I love you." CLICK.

Rita is quiet after she hears the click.

This is not how love flows through Rita, but Roberto lives in an entirely different reality. Over the years, Rita has learned to love beyond the limitations created by her mind and the mind of the collective. Some of those limitations are: you cannot love more than one person at a time; you can only love those things that you like; love doesn't hurt, it only feels good; you have to be perfect in order to be loved.

But Rita experiences love in a different way. Love is constant, it unifies, it does not separate, it does not judge, it allows for our humanness. It is the most powerful substance Rita experiences. Love is constantly expanding itself and its willingness to unify.

This is how Rita experiences the love that rises out of her heart. It is not how she experiences Roberto's physical form or her external connections with him. She is aware of his separation from love and it is Rita's experience that his ability to love does not change over time. The rigid structure of man's body, constructed out of his beliefs and thoughts, separates him from the source that lies within his own heart. Rita witnesses how her own life and relationships change through this loving flow, but also recognizes that it cannot change another. It cannot change the hardness of a person from the outside in. It is the flow of love from the inside out that transforms the hardness of structures. When a person exercises free will and says "yes" to love, choosing to unify rather than separate, he or she empowers the will of the heart. It is the will of the heart, aligned with Divine will, which transforms life. As Rita continues to reach out to the world with love from its genuine source within her, she is slowly and silently absorbed by this love. That is the purpose of the mantra, "Love No Matter What." One cannot gain love by an outer source; Divine Love must be absorbed cell by cell to produce change.

Rita tries to share this wisdom with Roberto, but his life, beliefs, culture, and body cannot accommodate this kind of love. In fact, most of the world cannot open itself to this Divine Love. It requires a person to say "yes" to love and all the changes that come from this creative force. Roberto does not differ from most people. He is part of the corporate world and has accepted their beliefs, their desires, and is living their "dream." The only difference is that Roberto has had a taste of something so real, so sweet that he begins to realize the emptiness of the choices he's made. Roberto knows what is real, but the external world pulls, bends and makes him into the man he is, separate from the Truth of his Being.

Roberto has had a direct experience with the Divine, but he continues to make choices based on the status quo of his life. For Roberto, nothing has changed in his life except his increasing disillusionment. He remains outwardly complacent, but a deep frustration and anger begins to surface. Rita places another call. Roberto answers. She hears noise in the background. Roberto is in another meeting. His voice is sharp and cutting. He says, "Diga me."

Rita is quiet then hangs up the phone. She has no further words. She feels his negativity cross the miles and touch the softness in her heart. Tears sting her eyes as she tries to surrender to the words, "Love No Matter What." Rita is acutely aware of her openness to love and the inability of other people in the physical world to allow that connection. Rita continues to breathe deeply, asking for Love to guide her. She does not retreat from the pain. She holds it beside Love within her heart. Rita realizes how much her heart has expanded over the years, grateful for every part of her experience with Roberto.

She crawls into bed with her husband and presses her face into his skin. She smells Chris's fragrance. Rita breathes him in so deeply that she absorbs his scent and it permeates her own skin. Rita feels gratitude for her partnership with Chris in every cell of her body. Rita is so grateful to be living and sharing time with a man that says "yes" to love and stays open to its changing current. Chris's experience with the ocean and wind help him to navigate the seas of Love with Rita.

The image of pulsing light in the center of the Earth is always in Rita's awareness. Rita shares this image with Chris and they synchronize their breath to the pulsing light. Their breathing begins to dissolve the illusion of separation that man has created with the planet that birthed his current form.

At breakfast Rita says, "Chris, can you give me an update on the oil spill in the gulf?"

Chris stays current on news through the Internet. Rita doesn't like to put her consciousness on these events, but reads them as outer signs of an inner process for the earth.

"They still haven't capped the oil leak," Chris reports in a low, sad voice.

"How many months has it been?"

"I think we are into the third month."

Rita feels the pain of the ocean, earth, and all the creatures that live in the sea as Chris reports on details about the spill. "You know that the greed at the center of this country will eventually destroy this planet. It is amazing that people remain unaware that in the end we are destroying that which supports our life."

Rita breathes out her pain.

Chris is quiet as they bear witness to the changes plaguing the world—businesses closing; people unable to sell their homes; a government offering bailout after bailout. No one speaks out to say, 'This current dream is over! Our greed and selfishness are killing the planet.' This greed and self-centeredness is a virus that infects every part of our thoughts, constantly directing us to consume that which has birthed us and supports us.

"You know, Chris," says Rita, "my experience with Roberto brought me many gifts. One of them is consciously witnessing the transformation of a man's self-centered ego that separated his physical body and earth from the Divine Spirit that dwells in all of life. It is painful to witness and experience what is occurring here on this planet, but it is so rich. The pain I feel is balanced with the Divine Love, which is so amazing, so endless, and bottomless." Rita looks into Chris's eyes.

"I feel that love is all around in our home and in our hearts as you speak," Chris says and reaches for Rita's hand. No more words are necessary. They allow their bodies to be breathed by the presence of Divine Love.

# The Preciousness of Life

Life itself is a delicate balance
Between Spirit and Matter

A point between

The inhalation and exhalation
Where creation itself lies

Waiting to be witnessed
Waiting to be known by the human heart

A fluid moment to be recognized

Realizing that it, too
Is part of the preciousness of life

Needing to be held
With the utmost care and tenderness

Illuminating the heart of gold in all of life.

It is four o'clock in the morning and Rita wakes up out of a deep sleep with a clear understanding of her childhood dream. She knows there are not two different worlds or planets in the dream; the worlds represent two states of consciousness being lived simultaneously on this planet. They only appear as two separate worlds with different operations and functions. In her dream, the dying planet represents the individuation of the self, the "me." It is represented in all aspects of current life even within the most sacred relationships. This consciousness identifies itself as "I" and relates to itself as separate from all others in the world. It is self-oriented and ego centered. The new consciousness being birthed is that of Oneness, where there is no separation and the "I" is replaced with ALL THAT IS. There is no relationship with the "self," only relationship to of life. The "self" no longer exists within the consciousness of ONENESS. The dilemma at the end of Rita's dream represents the two consciousnesses, that of self and that of Oneness. The consciousness of Oneness can hold the image of self, but within this consciousness it no longer exits.

The dream's technological, self-oriented world becomes so separate from the organic natural world that it no longer relates to the Earth as its Mother. It only knows itself as separate, orienting its reality around the consciousness of self rather than the global state of consciousness.

The center of the consciousness of Oneness is no longer about man; it turns around the Divine creative forces that are unified by LOVE. Rita feels the consciousness of Oneness and the consciousness of the individuated ego struggling with one another. The ego-centered consciousness resists the birth of the new consciousness of Oneness.

The birth of Oneness does not fit with the self-centered state currently being lived upon the earth. Rita looks back into her dream vision and sees a self-centered consciousness that leaves the planet unable to live the dream it has created. The self-centered consciousness separates itself from the Earth, no longer remembering it comes from her searches to discover another planet.

Rita feels the revelation of the Truth as a light of a different vibration entering into her mind, illuminating something she has not been able to see. In the dream, the self-oriented people who leave the planet Earth because it can no longer provide what they demand return to Earth. Rita now sees that they return because they are bound to her as their Mother. They are part of the earth and part of the current change of consciousness occurring within her. The current image is that man was birthed out of the earth. Rita sits with this awareness, allowing it to penetrate the dense thought forms that still inhabit her mind. A peaceful state settles her heart. She knows everything that is currently happening is divinely orchestrated and she feels it as beauty, as it takes place.

Rita contemplates this awareness. She sees quite clearly that the consciousness of humanity needs to move toward a global consciousness. This means that humanity knows the world is One Being and that all of life is part of that One Being. The choices being made should be for the whole of life, not self-interest. All of nature is pointing humanity in this direction, but most of humanity is unable to see the signs. The Internet is a clear sign of the interconnectedness of the planet and some are using it to assist this process. Other universal technologies such as Facebook and Twitter focus solely on the individual and have no global awareness.

Rita acknowledges that most of humanity is snoring, deep in sleep and unaware of the dream they are living. They have difficulty seeing that they are part of this dream and therefore part of the solution. Rita thinks about waking up from a deep sleep. When a person first opens their eyes, the eyes are unfocused, vision is blurry, the head foggy, the brain not quite alert. The body takes time to orient itself from a horizontal to a vertical plane. She wonders what it would mean to wake people from the world's current dream. Would they be shocked, disoriented, and try to hold on to what is known in their current dream through a state of fear?

Rita senses humanity can feel something is changing, but most are unaware that they are powerless to control it. Rita is amazed that people believe their lives will return to how they were ten years ago. The manipulation of the ego self is far-reaching. She cannot understand the human mind that is unable to see the evolution of life as it is occurring. Rita laughs at herself and thinks, "Well, if their eyes are still closed and they are caught in the dream, of course they cannot see."

After dressing, Rita walks outside to breathe in the cool ocean air. She loves the morning when the birds wake up singing to the rising sun. The dogs are always pumped for a walk down into the woods. They love to smell the scents of critters that passed by under the cloak of darkness. As Rita lets herself become one with the earth, she allows herself to sense with each step the life that is beneath her feet. A communication occurs without words. Rita's mind tries to interpret the communication, but no words conceptualize the experience.

Rita's mind takes her back to the end of the dream and its dilemma with the two worlds. Maybe it is the inability of her mind and its conceived ideas that is unable to see a way for the consciousness of humanity to change, and that is where the dream always ends.

As Rita continues to communicate nonverbally with the earth, a new question formulates: What if the dream is developing within the moment being lived? This means there would be no definite end to the dream because it is always currently unfolding, not something that needs to be fulfilled. Something being created at the same time it is being lived and experienced. This direct interaction with the earth and Rita takes place as she walks through the woods in a deep silence.

Rita listens to the question and her heart knows this is true. What has been an experience between two separate individuals, Rita and Roberto, is a direct experience of this new consciousness. Rita begins to sense her entire life has been leading to this place, in this time, which is being experienced by many. The childhood dream is being experienced now on the planet and it has an impact on her entire life. Rita does not understand all the inner workings of a mystical life, but she trusts this internal compass that guides her throughout her life. She trusts and experiences all the situations that life brings to her.

Rita walks up the hill that leads her back home. She witnesses that a profound experience and awareness has occurred between the earth, her heart and soul, and the Divine. Rita realizes the journey she is being pulled through exists within the human heart. It is amazing and beautiful like the ever-changing sunset. There are no words that can connect what is simultaneously being experienced and witnessed.

# Freedom

Beyond one's imagination
Beyond the sensate world
Is the place of endless possibilities

It exists beyond the horizons of our minds
It is new territory undiscovered
Unformed, preconceived

Most cannot reach this place
For they are bound by the manifest world of the known

They are not free within their hearts and minds
To soar above the constraints of beliefs and concepts

Those who have freed themselves
Can catch light upon the wings of their hearts

Bringing it down into the manifest world
Illuminating and nurturing the life force that exists within matter

Giving rise to a NEW WAY TO BE.

The mantra, "Love No Matter What" carries the image of Roberto through Rita's process. Rita's direct experience of Divine Love with another human being floats his image before her. The human part is experienced with the sensate body making the experience feel personal and intimate. The dualistic or individuated consciousness is what held the image of Roberto alive in Rita's mind until her heart eventually absorbed the image through Divine Love.

It is this deep trust of a presence of Love that can be directly experienced only through the human heart, which is what leads Rita on this journey. The workings within the human heart are available to those who seek beyond the frozen concepts of their minds. The love that is discovered begins to melt the concepts imprinted within the human mind. This makes it possible to move beyond the frozen limitations that have been created within the minds of men.

Rita keeps offering the journey to Roberto as she moves through it. The offerings are invitations to "Love No Matter What." Rita lives this reality with her partner, Chris. Chris's heart has opened with his "yes" to Love No Matter What. This allows love to flow through his heart, touching Rita's sensate body. This resonates with the Divine Love within her heart and returns back to Chris's sensate body, which completes a full breath cycle and an experience where the inner experience of Divine Love manifests into an outer experience.

And that is what Rita experienced with Roberto on the plane and in the airport. The invitation to "Love No Matter What" is extended to him over the years. His response to Divine Love within the physical form is met with conflict.

There is a "yes" within his heart but his mind is filled with preconceived ideas about Love. Slowly, his mind takes control and dominates his heart. Less and less love is exchanged between the sensate world and the spiritual world. This is mirrored in the interactions between Rita and Roberto.

The human heart is the doorway into the spiritual realm and opens from our willingness to "Love No Matter What," and to "Love Beyond Externalized Boundaries." It is the unification of Divine Love with the world of matter that threatens the frozen world of the ego. The fire of Divine Love burns through the longing heart, which melts the world of frozen conceived ideas. Rita now knows and witnesses the image of man himself as a conceived idea. This image manifests itself through the current dream being lived by humanity rising out of the earth herself.

Rita is in the kitchen preparing dinner. Chris loves to watch Rita in the kitchen. She glides across the bamboo floor; she chops and adds spices, creating a meal aligned with the rhythmic flow of life. The aromas rise from the stove, filling the room with a cornucopia of mouthwatering scents. The dogs lie on the floor, attempting to keep out of Rita's way, but close enough to watch for fallen morsels. Rita calls Chris to the table. They sit together with candles flickering between them. Chris reaches for Rita's hands and they give thanks for all they receive as an endless flow of love manifesting in their lives.

Rita looks at Chris and says, "The process I have been through with Roberto has brought much understanding and conscious richness to my soul. But it is your openness and your willingness to 'Love' that has made that consciousness manifest itself in our lives. I feel there were two things my soul wanted to experience in this lifetime: a direct and constant relationship with Divine Love, and a relationship with a man that manifests that love. My heart is so full with gratitude to have had both these experiences. You are such a beautiful man and are humble as you live your life. These qualities are so natural for you, Chris. The choices you make have a purity of innocence, which is what attracted me to you in the beginning."

Chris takes another bite of food and allows a moan of pleasure to escape his lips. He says, "I love you, too."

Rita doesn't need to hear words, for she feels the truth of them in her heart. Chris's actions are aligned with his words. The two become one flow without separation. "Honey," says Chris, "I don't always understand the words but I do understand something through our relationship and the interactions that flow between us."

"I know," Rita says and smiles at Chris with the warmth of the sun.

A silence fills the space between them as they share much more than words. In the silence Rita senses something that has no words, only the implication of completion, an ending of what is known giving rise to something that is unknown—a mystery. The dissolving of Roberto's image gives rise to the awareness of the Earth herself returning the image of mankind back to its Divine Essence. Earth is awakening to the consciousness of Oneness and in her awakening she no longer needs to hold the image of mankind in her soul. The Earth herself is free to return the image of mankind back to its Divine Source.

Rita has been holding the awareness of both states of consciousness her entire life. Rita and many others heard the cries of the earth, and they participate in the manifestation of Oneness through the current physical form. These individuals are pulled by a deep love they carry within their souls as they help illuminate the spark of Oneness contained within every human heart. It is this awakening that was contained in the original meeting between Rita and Roberto. Their direct and conscious experience through physical bodies helps in the reorganization of life currently occurring in the celestial body of Earth. It is Earth's awakening that humanity is witnessing when their hearts are open and they can see beyond the dividing concepts of the mind.

As human beings, we can participate in the process—consciously witnessing it as it occurs. As the flow of energies becomes stronger and changes take place, it is important to recognize that all things are held within the One Divine Being and absolutely nothing is separate within the consciousness of Oneness. Rita is aware this is a quantum leap for humanity. It will no longer be able to view life from the dualistic perspectives of "me" and "the other." She is also aware that those who are awake to the consciousness of Oneness assist all the rest through this evolutionary process. All of life is connected within a network of golden light. Nothing is separate. Rita witnesses this within her own life as the reality, even when she is caught in the illusion of separation through her own sensate body.

It has become clear to Rita that Roberto has been

affected by the direct experience of the energy of Oneness. Roberto continues to separate the two experiences and remain split by the two worlds—that of matter and that of Spirit. He is unable to bring them together within himself and within his life. Rita realizes the power of the current illusion that dominates humanity—most of humanity is ruled by fear. This idea continues to dominate and control the physical world, thinking of them and experiencing them as separate. Rita's heart continues to vibrate the words "Love No Matter What," continuing the experience of Oneness aligning with Divine Truth.

Rita has no clear vision of what the consciousness of Oneness looks like, for there are no concepts or images that can be held within the consciousness of Oneness. It is a flowing, timeless state of Being dynamically lived, experienced, and witnessed within the moment. Rita has been given glimpses of light as this consciousness rises from the depths of the human heart and from the soul of the earth.

Rita takes Chris's hand and they let the warmth of their palms heat together until their pulses glow. She knows their unified pulse reaches all of life, for there is nothing separate from the One Divine Being.

Rita reflects one last time on her dream of the two worlds—the one of Oneness and the other of separation. She no longer feels the dilemma that plagues the end of the dream or the dilemma she finds herself in when she meets Roberto. She realizes the consciousness of Oneness does not separate. The Earth herself now knows she is one with the Divine and all of life, no longer needing to hold the image of mankind that separates her from the Truth. During the journey, Rita inadvertently separated herself from Oneness when she identified herself as separate through her sensate experience of Divine Love. But as she continues through the process, everything, including the experience of Divine Love, becomes absorbed by Divine Love. There is no longer two, only one Divine Love that is witnessed. There are no more words that can bring humanity closer to its own True Essence.

# The Kiss

It started with the softest kiss
A melting, a spinning, a heating
Until everything that was known
Fell away

There was a grasping, a clawing
A contracting to keep what was known
To retain a sense of the self that had always been

Slowly and painfully
The sense of self changed and
Is no longer recognizable
The form it had taken
No longer exists.

A strange boundless freedom
Resting in a world of limited form
It is strange to be in this reality
When so many others appear to be trapped

The truth is no longer being reflected in the form
It is now being created within itself
There is an atmosphere of mystery
Of adventure, for nothing is familiar

The kiss has evolved

Beyond a man and a woman meeting
Into a union between form and formless
Light and shadow, depth and surface

No matter how one might insist upon a form
The universe is reordering itself
Nothing can remain the same
Nothing can remain unchanged

This journey started with...
Two individuals and now
There is only ONE
One flow, One movement, One Truth

Everything else has fallen away
Into its limited form, separate from the truth
Separate from the One thing that the kiss...
Was meant to awaken in the souls
Of mankind ................ LOVE.

Heidi Lorenz

# Epilogue

This is a time of great change upon the planet earth. Many global events have occurred to help awaken a shift in human consciousness. Humanity as a collective has not yet been able to bring about the balance between the masculine and feminine aspects. Largely this is dependent on the feminine aspect stepping forward—not against the masculine aspect, but to unify with the masculine.

This will take tremendous courage and strength and can happen only if women unify their efforts and reclaim the Power and Spirit of the Feminine. This is not dependent on the masculine; women must stop betraying the feminine aspect within themselves. And men must surrender to their own inner feminine aspect. This requires that men no longer see the feminine as an object they control, but as an equal partner unifying with that wisdom.

The possibility of union between the masculine and feminine aspects is what will lead humanity into Oneness and let it remain part of the current evolutionary process occurring on the planet. This must occur through the human heart. In the west, people's hearts have become trapped within their ego's desire, which disconnects them from the web of life that connects directly to the soul of the earth. Humans come from the earth. All indigenous people know this; without that connection, all of life suffers.

A great deal of Eastern and indigenous Spiritual wisdom has arrived in the West to assist with awakening this connection. Because the collective ego structure is so strong, much of the energy continues to be diverted back into old patterns and structures that are not life sustaining. These structures serve only individual stories and repetitive actions. They do not belong to the creative process currently being birthed by earth herself.

As these old structures based on greed, fear, and domination continue to fall away, they allow new possibilities can come through our hearts. When the ego, which divides matter from Spirit and masculine from feminine, is confronted with the Truth that all things are One, it no longer has power over humanity and the earth. This allows the healing force of love to move through matter in a new way, creating new possibilities. It creates something completely new that cannot be envisioned through current language and concepts. A new way to communicate with all of life can be born.

Rita and Roberto have been practicing this new form of communication without words, directly through their hearts. But such communication cannot be accomplished as long as the ego structure remains in its current position. A new dawn is rising, and what it will take is human beings aligning their personal will with the will of the Divine and say, "YES." Our choices are no longer about our self, but about the Whole of Life connecting us to the web of life that is breathed by the Divine. This writer's head bends in humility toward her heart, acknowledging that the Artistry of this life and all that it contains is the Divine breathing her.

# ADDITIONAL MATERIAL
## TO ASSIST UNDERSTANDING THE CONSCIOUSNESS OF ONENESS

The Diamond Approach and Ridhwan Foundation developed by
A.H. Almaas: **www.ahalmaas.com**

The Golden Sufi Center, teachings from the Naqshbandi Sufi
path: **www.goldensufi.org**

Working with Oneness website: **www.workingwithoneness.org**

Global TV: **www.linktv.org/globalspirit/oneness**

Books on Oneness by Llewellyn Vaughan-Lee:
> **www.goldensufi.org**
>> *Working with Oneness*
>> *Light of Oneness*
>> *Awakening the World*
>> *Spiritual Power: How It Works*
>> *The Return of the Feminine and the World Soul*

*The Unknown She: Eight Faces of an Emerging Consciousness*
by Hilary Hart: **www.unknownshe.org**

*In the Dark Places of Wisdom*
by Peter Kingsley

Many literary works and websites provide access for more information if you are ready to seek with your heart. Your heart will show you the way. If you need opening to access your body, then make the effort to do that with Yoga, Breath Work, Movement Classes, Massage and Body Work, dance, or whatever works for you. Maybe it is your mind that needs opening. If so, find ways to let go of the current concepts that hold you back through Art or dream work, journaling, or meditative practice. This is not a time to stand on the sidelines and watch. It is a time to participate fully in your life and know that it connects deeply to the whole of life!

**THE GIFT OF LIFE IS EVER PRESENT**

**BUT YOU NEED TO SAY YES!!!!!!!!**